SOUTHERN ELECTRIC DRIVER

*Driving trains during the final
years of slam door rolling stock*

Tim Wood

Capital Transport

This book is dedicated to my driving instructor Peter Hall and to the drivers and guards who made my time at Brighton so memorable.

I am greatly indebted to Ivan Wilson for providing invaluable information and for taking the time to read through this work with an expert eye and an unwavering enthusiasm. Thanks also to Paul Edwards, Ashley Barton, Adrian Durrant, Tony Harper and my very patient family, Claire, Emma and Tom. This book could not have been written without their support and inspiration.

A website has been compiled by drivers Paul Edwards and Ivan Wilson. 'The Brighton Motive Power Depots' contains invaluable stories and photographs which chart the history of the Brighton footplate men. Connected websites incorporate the stories of the Sussex motive power depots and the Brighton branch of ASLEF. The website address is: http://thebrightonmotivepowerdepots.yolasite.com

The EPB Preservation Group is currently working to restore 4 CEP 7105, 2 EPB 5759 and a selection of motor luggage vans. The group are based on the East Kent Railway at Shepherdswell and more details can be found at www.epbpg.co.uk

I have used the enduring term 'Southern Electric' because it is affectionately and commonly used, by train crews and enthusiasts alike, for all designs of electric multiple unit that have run in any period over the former Southern Region railway network.

First published 2014

Published by Capital Transport Publishing Ltd
www.capitaltransport.com

Printed by Parksons Graphics

© Tim Wood 2014

Front cover: The vast majority of 'Capital Coast Express' services, which ran between Victoria and Brighton, were driven by link three Brighton drivers. 8 DIG unit number 2003 is seen on the down fast line at Stoat's Nest Junction, just south of Purley, on one such service in March 1994. *Alex Dasi-Sutton*

Contents

Introduction

For many years I have been a great admirer of railways. Love them or loathe them, the railways of Britain have provided an excellent service to millions of people for well over a hundred years. The engineering involved is on a gargantuan scale. The design of the infrastructure, buildings and trains which the Victorian engineers kindled was the beginning of an ever evolving network, which to this day, constantly adapts to our needs in this very modern world. Take a look around any transport book shop and you will see hundreds, possibly thousands, of volumes covering all manner of things 'Railway'. Locomotives probably have more books written about them than any other subject. They are followed closely by books about wagons, coaches, railway companies and so on.

I have digested these books over the years and, like many people across the country, have been inspired by the actual trains themselves. The 'Flying Scotsman', High Speed Trains, day to day multiple units, freight trains, all have their own appeal. There are many subjects within the story of the railways which can capture people's imagination. Therefore, there is a wide and varied amount of enthusiasts out there, all with their own particular interests concerning railways.

I have, however, noticed that there are very few accounts of what it is actually like to drive trains on a day to day basis. There are of course stories of famous runs which include the driver of *Mallard* breaking the world speed record with somewhat 'on the edge' bravado being applied to achieve this. Steam and diesel drivers' tales occasionally turn up in railway magazines but these are few and far between. There seems to be a lot of printed matter concerning timetables and locomotive performance but there is very little material available which describes how trains are actually driven! This could just be because the subject has not yet been attempted.

My time as a train driver did not involve racing at 100mph on a Deltic or flogging a Stanier pacific up Shap. It covered a period that has not, as far as I know, been written down for posterity. I know that electric trains are not everybody's 'bag' but the slam door stock which I spent my time on has now gone, just like steam and most of the pioneering diesel traction. If this knowledge is forgotten because nobody has taken the time to write it down, then it, like so many things before, will be lost forever. This, more than anything else, is what has inspired me to write this account. Although I have included a few photos of multiple units, this book is not intended to be a photographic study of trains. I have, however, included a 'further reading' section which lists photographic publications that are relevant to the text. There is also a list of available DVDs which can give the reader a glimpse of what it is like to drive trains, and in particular, what it is like to drive slam door stock on the Southern Region. A lot of this book has been written from memory and any mistakes included are purely of my own making!

I have been employed by the railway on two separate occasions. I worked as a member of platform staff for a few years and then, after a short break, I worked as a driver. I have written about my platform experience in chapter one. I have been lucky enough to have a fairly rounded career on the railway and in hindsight it was good to have more knowledge of how the system worked before actually climbing into the cab. I also spent a short time on work experience in Newhaven Harbour signal box.

As a young lad I grew up in Addiscombe which is a satellite town of Croydon. I was fortunate enough to have the Mid-Kent line at the bottom of my garden. My house backed on to the crossover that led into Addiscombe carriage shed. In the evenings, commuter trains from London would run past the bottom of the garden and into the station. They would then come back out past a shunt signal. The driver would then run the train over the crossover and in to the shed for the night. The same would happen, but in the reverse order, for the morning peak. This would occur, at each end of the day, with four or five trains in quick succession. Occasionally, I would watch the proceedings from high in our old damson tree. This afforded a better view because the embankment which carried the line was fairly high. The only trains that went past between the peak hours were the 2 EPB Elmers End shuttles. These connected with London bound trains which originated from Hayes, Kent. The shuttles were locally known as 'sixpenny bumpers'.

On two or three occasions, when I was growing up in the late sixties and early seventies, the daily humdrum of watching trains going through the motions was interrupted by a loud bang. This was accompanied by a bright flash if it was dark. The upshot of this was that a train had de-railed on the crossover because it had, perhaps, been taken too quickly! The result usually left an EPB unit leaning precariously over our garden! The flash came from the live rail as it was shorted out by a wheel or bogie. More than once, my Dad emptied anything of value out of the shed, just to be on the safe side. Annoying as this was to my parents, it meant that I would usually get to watch a class 33 arrive with a breakdown crane. I would then stay up for half of the night to watch the re-railing operation. The noise of the Crompton, the crane, and a lot of shouting from people, who were desperate to get the obstruction out of the way before the morning rush hour, was not the best remedy for a child who had insomnia anyway. The excitement however did

2 EPB 6275 was derailed whilst running through the crossover into Addiscombe carriage shed in the early 1990s. This illustration shows the unit being assisted by a breakdown crane which was brought to the scene by class 33 'Crompton' 33 212. *Laurence Budd*

fire my interest in railways. I was also lucky enough to have a great aunt who lived in a block of flats which was directly above the line between East Croydon and Windmill Bridge Junction. From the seventh floor there was a great view in all directions and I would sit on the kitchen table watching lots of SUBs, EPBs and 1963 stock. The occasional Brighton Belle would also pass through. My great uncle had worked as a wheel tapper at Selhurst depot which was just along the road from the flats. He was as deaf as a post by the time he retired and he had no interest whatsoever in trains!

I had a very close shave, in a small playground opposite this block of flats, when I was about ten years old. I remember that it had swings, a slide and a witch's hat which would probably be deemed far too dangerous for children these days! The playground was divided from the railway by a high brick wall and I managed to kick a football, which belonged to some older boys, over the wall and on to the track. After some deliberation, I was elected to go over and retrieve it! I didn't really think that I had much choice because the boys were twice my size. Using a park bench for a leg up, I made my way up the corner of the wall. There were bushes on the right hand side and in front of me there were five tracks, all with live rails! To put it mildly, I was in a no-win situation ... I would still have to get back over the high wall if I survived retrieving the ball! Poised for the drop to the other side and scared out of my wits, my life was saved by a 4 SUB unit which came around the curve on the closest track! I'm not sure if I fell or jumped back into the playground but I landed on the tarmac with a hard bump! I now realise that this line was the down slow and I never drove along it without thinking that I would not be here if it was not for that 4 SUB! I wouldn't have got away with it if I had jumped a second or two earlier. The boys in the playground, probably realising the enormity of what had 'nearly' happened, decided it was best that a second attempt to retrieve the ball would not be sensible. This was a good thing because there was no way that I was going to try again. I was ready for an attempt to outrun the boys if the decision had gone the other way!

My great aunt's sister, i.e. my grandmother, worked in Newmark's factory which overlooked the line adjacent to Windmill Bridge Junction. She often used to tell me of the time that she had been gazing out of the window only to see a member of the permanent way staff killed by stepping on to the live rail. She had a vivid memory of his hair catching fire! Terrible for the poor fellow but a brilliantly gripping story for a young lad! I sometimes cycled the short distance from Addiscombe to Tennison Road Bridge which offered a commanding view over Norwood yard and Selhurst depot. This was the Central Division's stronghold for the steel bodied 4 SUBs and there was always something interesting to look at. De-icing units, formed from earlier rolling stock, were usually visible and on one occasion there was a Western class diesel locomotive idling near the fuelling point, a bit of a rarity on the Southern. There were sidings beyond the London Bridge line and these contained some condemned wooden bodied units. At the far end of the bridge was a park which was situated adjacent to the carriage washing machine. Any number of units would run through this on their way into the depot and if it was windy you could get a fair shower as the flails spun at great speed! My house was only a mile or so from the main line and on still, icy nights I could hear loose-coupled wagons clanking into each other while my bedroom walls were illuminated by distant arcing from electric trains running between East Croydon, Selhurst and Norwood Junction. My room was level with the line at the bottom of the garden and the EPBs gave some terrific crackling light shows as the last trains of the day negotiated the crossover into the shed.

I was taken on a daytrip to France at the age of eleven. We didn't have a car so we caught a bus to Bromley South and then went by train to Dover Priory. A great time was had by all and something unexpected happened at the end of the day. It was fairly late at night when I complained to my Mum that we had been sitting on the train at Dover for ages and wasn't it about time that we got moving? To my great surprise, two men dressed in railway uniform poked their heads around from the next row of seats and introduced themselves as the driver and guard of our train. They'd been having a chin-wag and a cuppa before setting off for the journey. To my amazement, the driver looked just like Eric Morecambe, large, thick framed glasses included. He invited me up to the cab, plonked me in the driver's seat and said, "Do you want to have a drive then?" So there I was in the cab of 4 CEP, unit number 7182, with a kind man offering me a dream come true on a plate! I nodded nervously and we set off. I don't remember much about the journey, only that it was frighteningly dark inside and outside of the cab. No head-lights were fitted in those days and I couldn't understand how the driver could know where we were. We arrived at Canterbury East and the driver said that he would take over because the train was going to be attached to another one at Faversham. I remained in the cab until we pulled up tight to another 4 CEP unit. The driver said that my Mum would be wondering where I had got to so I thanked him with all my heart and walked back down the train with a beaming smile and a rather stiff right arm. This was caused by holding the deadman's handle down for so long. The driver had told me not to let go of it because if I did the train would come to a very hard stop. I clung on for dear life though I am sure that he had hardly let go of the handle or the brake valve during the whole journey. Originally, CEP deadman's handles were set at 7lb/psi so were a little tough to hold down for long periods anyway. The CEPs were fitted with the later style of handle when they were refurbished in the 1980s. These operated at 4lb/psi which must have been more comfortable for the drivers. With a feeling of elation and a little disbelief as to what had just taken place, I informed my family that 'I' had driven the train all by myself! In truth, I hadn't really understood how I had done it but I knew that I was hooked. From then on, I knew that I wanted to be a train driver when I grew up.

We moved to Seaford on the Sussex coast in my mid teens and in 1985 I landed myself a job on the platform at Lewes station. This was a great start for a keen railway enthusiast. There were still lots of old hands on the sta-tion and they were full of fantastic tales which involved gory, often heroic, railway happenings. There were ghosts which allegedly haunted the station! These stories were of course related to the younger members of staff on the quieter night turns, more of which later. I gradually learned the ropes and settled into the routine of the day to day running of the station. After a while I put in an application for a second man's job at Brighton. This involved a quick interview with the train crew manager which was followed by a short mathematics test. After a few days I was called into Brighton and formally offered the position. I turned the offer down because the wages turned out to be about half of what I could earn on the station, which wasn't that much anyway. I soon became disheartened and left the railway to work as a post-man with the Royal Mail. My delivery route followed the railway line from Seaford towards Bishopstone and it did not take long before I realised that I had made a dreadful and rather short-sighted mistake! I missed the railway terribly and watching the trains go by was like rubbing salt into a wound. I stayed with the Post Office for six years but the drudge of posting letters was not for me. I saw an advertisement and applied for the position of 'Trainman D' (trainee train driver). I was lucky enough to secure myself a job and I started my new career at Brighton depot in the February of 1994.

Brighton had a link of about twenty Trainmen Ds who were all waiting patiently for a driving course. The first course that we were sent on was guard's rules so that we could fill in on 'bell ringing' turns. Brighton always seemed to suffer from a constant shortage of guards. Luckily, it was still a mixed traction depot so we were required to cover ballast work duties at weekends and on night turns. This helped to break the monotony of guarding on passenger trains and it was good to go out with a top link driver and get a bit of loco hauled experience. The top link men were all trained on diesels and alongside ballast duties they worked class 47s on the 'Sussex Scot' and Cross Country services to Manchester. There were pilot turns which involved the resident Lover's Walk class 09s. These locomotives were usually referred to as '350s' by drivers because this was the amount of horsepower that they could muster. They were used for hauling the class 47s and their rolling stock up to Top Yard where the 47s would run round on to the London end. The 350 would then haul the train back into the station. On the engineering side, the traction would usually consist of classes 33, 37 or class 73 electro-diesels. The top link men also had traction knowledge of the de-icer/sandite units which were utilised throughout the autumn and winter months.

I gained an immeasurable amount of experience from the older drivers over the course of about eighteen months. They had a huge combined wealth of knowledge which they were only too glad to pass on to the younger novices. Some fun was had too and a bit of good humoured teasing would occasionally cause some merriment in the mess room. I remember a certain driver smiling, waving a filthy pair of hands in my face and adding the comment; "You see that. That's diesel grease that is. You won't ever get that on your hands!" The 'dinosaurs', as they became affectionately known, nicknamed the trainman Ds 'microwaves' or 'boil in the bag' drivers. It had taken them a long time to make the footplate grade and in the modern world a man off the street could be trained as a driver in under two years. It must be remembered that no human being is above making a mistake due to human error. Occasionally, an older and more experienced driver would make a slip up which would leave them wide open for a bit of ribbing!

A certain senior driver took a wrong signal aspect when leaving Brighton with a Thameslink service. When heading for the main line towards London the theatre box above the signal displayed an 'M'. Unfortunately, this driver pulled out of the station with an 'E' on the signal. The 'E' stood for 'East Coastway' and the 319 unit ended up running on to the London Road viaduct, via Montpelier Junction. The driver shunted the unit back into Brighton and, with some delay, re-started the journey to Bedford. Naturally, an anonymous wag posted a hilarious route diagram on the mess room wall. It demonstrated how to get on to the mainline from the station throat in easy to follow steps! The driver concerned took the ribbing in good humour and, needless to say, never did it again!

The derelict remains of Seaford's train crew depot which is situated opposite the one remaining station platform. *Author*

Sadly, during my time at Brighton, all ballast work was lost to EWS and the class 47 work was lost to Virgin Trains. This left just an early and late turn pilot duty for the diesel men. The Thameslink services were also lost to a new dedicated depot which was based in a separate building at Brighton. Twenty-six drivers transferred to it on the day it opened.

Brighton was an excellent depot but I was originally hoping to get a position at Seaford. Unfortunately, this little depot closed about two weeks before I started on the job. Until this time, Seaford crews had booked on by phone to the train crew supervisor in Brighton. It was decided to close the smaller depots because the T.C.S. could not physically see that men were fit for duty when signing on for a shift. Most of the Seaford drivers and guards were dispersed between Brighton and Eastbourne. Amazingly, one of the Seaford drivers had been at Addiscombe depot when I lived there. I talked to him about the various derailments which had occurred on the crossover behind my old house. He informed me that it could have had something to do with the drivers hurrying to get their trains in to the shed and their bodies into the Alma Tavern which was just near the station! Apparently, the Addiscombe to Elmers End shuttles were often run on a dodgy kind of shift pattern. The driver would take a return shuttle while the guard was in the pub. The guard would then do the next run while the driver was in the pub! It was worth waiting many years to be enlightened with this information!

I eventually moved far enough up the seniority list to get on a driver's rules course. This was closely followed by a traction course on 1963 stock. The '63 stock, as it was generally known, comprised of four-car CIG, BIG and VEP units. During my early days as a driver, a few sets of CIGs and BIGs were semi-permanently coupled to form 8 DIG units. These were used on the hourly 'Capital Coast Express' Brighton to Victoria 'fast' services which only stopped intermediately at East Croydon. I remember being roughly thrown around in the brake van when working as a guard on one of these units. The driver seemed to think that 90mph on a 75mph stretch of track would go unnoticed as we approached Preston Park which was only a short hop from Brighton. For a brief moment it flashed through my mind that I may have to make the uncomfortable decision to 'drop the handle' on another member of staff! The speed eventually came down very hard as we approached the gradually lowering restrictions of 40, 25 and finally 15mph into the platforms. This driver was a bit of a racer and I quickly found out that you normally had to wait for time at stations if he was up the front. The very same man was promoted to the grade of traction inspector within a year of this incident. Rather ironically, he would occasionally be seen with a speed gun out on Montpelier Junction!

Speed guns were most often used outside termini because low speed restrictions were in place through the crossovers and on approach to the buffer stops. A driver was allowed 3mph on either side of the limit. One mph was allowed for the gun, one for the driver and one for the speedometer. More than 3mph in excess of the speed restriction would result in disciplinary action being taken. This was bearing in mind that trains were driven at the speed limit, wherever possible, so as to keep to the timetable. There was not much room for error!

The CEPs came to Brighton just a short time after I had signed the route to Victoria. There were seven units which were all borrowed from the South Eastern Division. All were in a very poor state and it had been a long time since any had seen a paintbrush. Since driving 7182 as a child, I had given up hope of ever getting the chance to drive a CEP again. I had always had them down as my favourite units, and years before when I worked on the platform at Lewes, I had made a point of watching the morning and evening Newhaven boat trains trundle through the station. The motors would hum softly as the driver applied a little power to keep the train from losing momentum through the sharp curve. These were the only CEP workings which came through Lewes at that time. They were always formed of eight coaches with an additional motor luggage van at the London end. As for driving them at Brighton, it wasn't to be! There were only a few diagrams which utilised them. The roster clerk only needed so many men to be trained on them and I wasn't far enough up the seniority list to get on a traction conversion course. This was, to say the least, disappointing but as luck would have it, I was asked to work a rest day as a guard, ringing the bell for drivers who were on the CEP conversion course. Normally a passed driver would sneer at such a proposition but it was a chance at least to work with one of my favourite units. The drivers were bored after a couple of hours taking turns at the controls. There were still a few hours to go and the instructor, who just happened to be the man who had passed me out for driving, asked if I would be interested in having a drive myself. At last, an offer that I couldn't refuse! I managed to drive all the way from Brighton to Littlehampton and then back to Brighton. Things felt as if they had come full circle after many years of patience. I never did get the chance to drive a CEP on my own but at least this time I had had a fair idea of what I was doing when placed in the driver's seat!

Lewes

WORK EXPERIENCE IN NEWHAVEN HARBOUR SIGNAL BOX

My first taste of life on the railway came very quickly after I left school. My father managed to secure me a few days on 'work experience' in Newhaven Harbour signal box. This was a fairly small box but it controlled movements on to the single line which then headed off towards Bishopstone and Seaford. It also controlled movements into the Newhaven Marine platform and sidings where trains connected with the Dieppe ferry.

I was first shown how to enter a train's passing in the train register and then I spent a couple of hours observing the proceedings before being allowed to actually get involved in the running of the box. Under the signalman's guidance I worked out which signal and point levers needed pulling for a particular move. The illuminated diagram above the levers helped although the signalman only ever referred to this when he needed to know if a train was approaching his section. Next I was taught to contact the signal box at Newhaven Town by using bell codes. The bell was rung when either accepting a train 'from' or sending trains 'to' the Newhaven Town section. This was all fairly simple and after a while the signalman let me work the box without much interference. He only interceded if I had omitted to do things in the right order.

I learned the basics of signalling and only made one small mistake! There was a home signal which protected the junction when a train approached from the Seaford direction. This signal was about a quarter of a mile from the box and at first it took a fair bit of pulling. I was taught that technique was far better than brute strength when pulling levers. Eventually I got the hang of it but not before I had had a driver yell at me from his cab window as he coasted past the box. I had failed to pull the signal on the first attempt and I watched it bounce a couple of times before restoring to the danger position. I got it at the second attempt but not before the driver had slowed his train down for no reason other than my lack of skill. I fully deserved the mouthful that he gave me! The signalman smiled and reassuringly said that I would get the hang of it. Having been a train driver, I now know just how irritating it can be to be slowed by a signalman who wasn't doing his job efficiently.

Newhaven Harbour signal box. The Marine platform lines are nearer to the box and the Seaford lines are nearer to the camera. *Author*

RAILMAN'S DUTIES AT LEWES

I worked in a couple of dead end jobs before securing a position as a junior railman at Lewes station. My appointment was swiftly followed by various courses which were mostly held in a portacabin at Brighton. Initially, health and safety courses were covered. These involved learning simple tasks such as track walking and crossing lines. There was one rule in place that was particularly important to follow when track walking on the Southern Region. I was taught to always step from ballast to ballast. Sleepers could be slippery, but more importantly, if you avoided treading on any rails, you lowered the chances of inadvertently treading on the conductor rail! This was followed by a basic signalling and shunting course where I learned how to attach and detach multiple units. I was also taught how to couple and uncouple loco hauled stock. This completed, I then learned that the platform staff also carried out hand signalling in the area when fixed signals had failed. I was taught how to operate level crossings manually by the station supervisor. This was required if a crossing failed and could not be worked electrically by track circuit or signal box. Occasionally, we would also work them when the line was closed for engineering work. This involved lowering and raising crossing barriers and then hand signalling or lamping the trains over the crossing. Within a week of passing out on level crossings I spent two days at Hamsey automatic half barriers in heavy snow. Funny how the junior member of staff had to go out when it failed in poor weather! Point winding was also part of the job. Occasionally in bad weather the points at Southerham Junction would fail. This could be a slow and laborious task where more time would be spent on the phone to the signalman than actually winding the points over. Once completed, trains would be flagged or lamped over the junction at caution.

As a junior railman I looked after platforms 3, 4 and 5 which were on the 'Branch' as it was known. Trains running through from Brighton, Seaford, Eastbourne and Hastings were my department and I had to make train announcements with a small microphone which was located in a cabinet on platform 3. This took some getting used to when performing in front of the public and people would regularly try to ask questions while you were in mid-announcement! The leading and senior railmen covered the London platforms 1 and 2. There was also a station supervisor whose job it was to see the back end of London trains away because of the tight curve on these platforms. Other duties included sweeping up on the platforms and in the waiting rooms, loading and unloading mail bags and Red Star parcels and also collecting and delivering lockable, leather cash bags. These were sent from the booking office and were delivered around the system by train. Each bag was signed for by every person who handled it during its journey. The grubbiest job of all was clearing litter from the track. This was done on the night turn and involved wearing heavy duty rubber gloves because the conductor rail was always 'live' even though the signals were set at danger to protect us.

THE CUCKOO GUARD

Seeing the trains out of the platforms was usually a straightforward affair. You would check the time and look up the stairs to see that nobody was heading for the train and then raise one arm to let the guard know that platform duties were complete. A certain guard was a little unpopular with us platform staff because he got grumpy when his train was held up for any reason. He was known for being a 'cuckoo' guard. That is to say, he would poke his head out of the door and as soon as he got the 'right away' from the platform he would ring 'two on the bell' informing the driver that it was ok to proceed. He would then close his door and disappear as if he had more important things to do, just like a cuckoo in a Swiss clock! On slam door stock, the guard was meant to see the train right out of the platform, just in case anybody tried to board or alight while the train was pulling away. 'One on the bell' was the signal for the driver to stop immediately.

On one afternoon, this very same guard was working a down Seaford train. I had checked the stairs and raised my arm to give the 'right away.' In what seemed like the blink of any eye, a woman who was aged about forty, hurtled down the stairs and ran for the train as it began to move. I firmly told her to "Stand clear!" but she reached out for a door handle and slipped, landing on her bottom with the lower half of her legs hanging down over the platform edge. I threw both arms up (the standard railway hand signal for 'Stop') but could not stop the train because the guard had done his disappearing act. There was nothing that I could do but stand by the lady and tell her not to move.

Platform 3 is on a bit of a curve and I stood there hoping that her clothes would not catch on the running boards and her knees and feet would not be hit by the axle boxes or bogie fittings. The woman looked petrified but did just as I had said and froze. I think that there would have been more chance of a nasty accident if I had tried to pull the lady backwards onto the platform. Due to the curves and junction, the speed limit through Lewes on the branch has long been a very cautious 10mph. Back in those days, most drivers, including this one, would just open the power up and go for it, knowing that they would soon be over the junction where the speed limit climbed to 40mph. The train must have been moving at about 25mph by the time that the rear coach had passed. I was in a cold sweat and I cannot imagine what must have been going through this poor lady's head! My station supervisor, on hearing me shout, had looked over and had seen the whole incident unfold. I yelled at the woman out of sheer panic. "What the bloody hell do you think you were doing? You could have got yourself killed!" The lady was shaking and I helped her up as she burst into tears and began to apologise profusely. I then felt bad for upsetting her. She had been through enough already for one day and she just kept saying "Sorry, I promise I won't do it again!" The supervisor reported the guard to the control room for not seeing his train away. It could have been very serious and it had been lucky that the lady wasn't badly hurt or even killed. We comforted her for a while, until she had got over the shock, then she caught the next available train home. We assumed that the guard would have been in for a severe reprimand.

Guards would see their own trains away when on an up working departing from platform 4. The curve on this platform is concaved and trains were rarely longer than four coaches so a good view could be had along the whole length of the train. Platform 3, being on a convex curve, was always staffed to see trains away because the guard could not see the front and rear from his position in the centre of a four coach train. The platform staff however, could see the guard at all times and were thus able to stop the train with a hand signal should the need arise.

We later realised that the 'cuckoo' guard had indeed been disciplined. He had begun to make a point of phoning across to ask for platform staff to see him away when leaving platform 4, which as stated above, was totally unnecessary! He would hold up the train until somebody arrived to do the honours and would report the platform staff to 'Control' for delaying the train. This went on for a few months and things became a little tense. He had taken the disciplinary as a personal criticism and not as a lesson in safety. After a while he went back to being a cuckoo so we really had to keep an eye out for him. Later on, as a driver, I would always look back out of the cab side window until the rear of my train had cleared a platform. Most guards were very conscientious. The incentive for disappearing was usually to gain the five percent commission from selling tickets on board.

FOG

An interesting incident happened in the time that some of the older station staff had been at Lewes. In earlier days, the Uckfield line ran out and across a viaduct which spanned the main high street. A fellow who worked the platforms alongside our oldest member of staff went out on to the viaduct to refill a signal lamp with oil. It had been reported as 'extinguished' by a driver. The night was foggy and so it was important to refill the lamp quickly. The man was away from the station for an unusually long time so his mate went towards the station throat to look for him. He found him crawling along the track and he was carrying the lower half of his leg! He had been hit by a coasting tank engine; the fog had muffled the sound of its approach. The man survived his ordeal and, from that day on, an old fashioned kettle was always on the stove so that boiling water was at hand in case of future emergencies. The kettle was tended by the man who related the story to me and he protested loudly every time the station master rebuked him for wasting British Rail's gas supply!

I had a bit of a fright myself one morning when returning to Lewes from point winding at Southerham Junction. It was foggy and I was walking in the down road cess, facing the direction of traffic as it stated that you must do in the rule book. The fog was extremely thick as I walked over the limited clearance bridge which crossed the river Ouse. A 3D 'Oxted' thumper unit, which was on the 'up' road, came hurtling across the bridge from behind me. It too was coasting and although these units were pretty noisy, even with the power shut off, I never heard it until it was next to me. If I had been on the 'up' road I doubt that I would be writing this book! When learning to walk the track I was warned that electric trains were often seen before they were heard so it made sense to be doubly aware in limited visibility. These incidents certainly seem to back up this warning.

The country end of Lewes station. From left to right are platforms 5, 4, 3, 2 and 1. The three Brighton branch platforms are on the left, while the London lines veer away to the right. *Author*

GHOSTS

There was a rumour at Lewes that long ago a man had been murdered by being pushed out of a train in the tunnel. Although I tried, I never could find evidence to back this up. That said, I was involved with a strange incident which concerned the 396yd-long tunnel. I had just booked on at 2.00pm for a late turn and was in the process of swapping over with the early shift. All members of staff were in the supervisor's office when a member of the public urgently called us out on to the concourse. This gentleman was in a bit of a fluster and he relayed to us that he had just seen an old man walk down the platform ramp and straight into the mouth of the tunnel. He had not come back out. The supervisor immediately phoned the signalman and arranged a 'block' to be put on the London lines. Safe in the knowledge that red signals protected both ends of the tunnel, four of us grabbed our Bardic hand lamps and we began to run along to the London end of platform 2. The arrival of a Victoria train was imminent and the platform was busy. At least three separate parties called out to us that we should hurry because the man had only recently entered the tunnel. One person stated that the man was very old and can't have got too far. We were at the tunnel mouth within two minutes of receiving the message. Two of us took the up line and two the down. We worked along the tunnel methodically and steadily, searching all of the refuges on the way. The tunnel was quite dark due to the curve at the station end but we rounded it pretty quickly. Nobody could have been out of the other end by the time that the far portal came into view. We reached this after a few minutes and if there had been somebody there we would have seen their silhouette ahead of us. We searched beyond the tunnel to no avail, there were no gates and the fences were of the standard six foot high 'wire' type. We slowly walked back through the tunnel, systematically searching the refuges as we went. We found nothing so we repeated the whole process but still to no avail. The London train was waiting in the platform and had been delayed by about thirty minutes. After some deliberation, it was allowed to proceed through the tunnel at caution. People were still insisting that the old man had walked in at a slow pace and had not reappeared at the station end. I cannot, to this day, explain what had happened that afternoon but there were plenty of witnesses as to what had taken place. It certainly made me think for a bit and has always stayed with me. Could a paranormal explanation be possible? I don't think a physical explanation would cover this incident and I'm not sure that I believe in ghosts but after many years of thought I still cannot come up with a solution.

A similar experience occurred after I had been promoted to leading railman. The mess room and offices were directly below the overbridge which connected all of the platforms with the booking office at the front of the station. I was working on a night turn with a senior railman, and having locked the station after the last train had departed, we finished the sweeping up and retired to the mess for a hot drink and something to eat. At about 2.30am we quite clearly heard footsteps on the bridge above us. They moved from one end of the ceiling to the other. Normally we were used to this sound but not in the small hours and well after lock up. There was a permanent way gang that was based at Lewes but they had gone out on a job and weren't due to return until morning. There should have been nobody else on the station. The mess room was situated below the bridge at roughly halfway between the London and branch platform stairs. We both jumped out of our seats and split up; my mate took the London stairs and I took the stairs on the branch side. We hurried, thinking that we were going to meet vandals or a trespasser. We met in the middle of the bridge within moments of hearing the footsteps. There was nobody to be seen! The ramp to the platforms was empty and the door into the ticket hall was locked. The identity of whoever, or whatever, had caused the footsteps was never revealed. That may well have been a good thing! I worked on night shifts on one week out of three and occasionally on my own at weekends. I am very glad to say that I only had one experience of inexplicable phenomena at night! I mentioned it to the late turn men on the next evening and they laughed and said it must have been one of the many ghosts that haunted the station! One of the old hands said that it was probably the ghost of a monk due to the fact that the station was built on top of the remains of Lewes Priory. It is true that some of the Priory was demolished to make way for the station but the footsteps that we heard were of somebody wearing much heavier footwear than open-toed leather sandals!

Lewes tunnel is situated at the northern end of the London platforms.
Author

BRUTES

Occasionally we had some fun with the British Rail Universal Trolley Equipment which was more commonly known as the B.R.U.T.E. These heavy and unwieldy movers of newspapers, parcels and mail bags had poor brakes and steered like supermarket trolleys. On night turns we would haul them to the top of the ramp which connected the overbridge with the platforms. We would then hang on to one and see who could get back to the bottom in the shortest amount of time. A modern health and safety man would, I'm sure, have put an end to this kind of fun! These trolleys were always parked out of the way and parallel to the platform edge with the brake applied. On one occasion a BRUTE did somehow roll on to the track. It took five men to manhandle it back on to the platform. Luckily it did not do any damage to the track although it narrowly missed the live rail!

SIGNAL BOX WINDOWS

Returning to normal station duties, one of the tasks of the junior railman was to go to the box on Friday mornings to clean the windows, inside and out. When the sun was shining this was quite a nice job and sometimes, if the windows were not too dirty, the signalman would give you a drink and a demonstration of how to work the panel. The signalmen did however insist on the windows being washed with hot, soapy water which would then be dried with elbow grease and newspaper. At this time it was still the signal-man's duty to check that a train was displaying the correct headcode and tail lights and some insisted that they could not do this properly unless the windows were absolutely sparkling. I once arrived at the box with a window cleaner's 'squeegee' so as to make a quick and easy job of it. I was told not to use it in no uncertain terms! In poor weather this task was laborious and could also be a little hair-raising when cleaning the outside of the glass. If a train was routed through the platform 5 loop it would pass just beneath you and the railing on the slippery walking board around the box was, to say the least, quite low and very fragile! Most of the signalmen were very professional but we would quite often get a relief man who could be very unpredictable. He was nicknamed 'God' because he would divert local trains into the wrong platform without informing us first. This was quite unhelpful and passengers had to be directed over the bridge to the reversible loop plat-form which would inevitably cause unnecessary delays. Our regular signalmen sometimes helped us out on nights by giving us a call before the first train in the morning, thus allowing us to have forty winks if things were quiet. There was, at this time, a bell on the station concourse which the signalman would ring to warn us of the approach of a train. Naturally some commuters had worked out the codes and would react accordingly on hear-ing the bell ring for their particular train.

Overleaf Lewes signal box. The London lines are on the left while the Brighton branch comes in from the right. *Author*

ATTACHMENTS AND DETACHMENTS

Eventually you got used to running the odd risk but just occasionally you got more than you bargained for! When splitting a train into two on platform 1 the units usually had the pipes and jumper cable connected on the platform 'nearside.' Each evening the 'split', as it was known, came down from Victoria and divided at Lewes with one portion bound for Seaford and the other bound for Eastbourne. On one particular evening I had to go 'offside' to undo the connections. Whilst standing on the step plates between the units, one foot on each, a London bound train pulled into platform 2 and stopped immediately behind me. This was fairly unnerving as I had to complete my duties quickly and then stay where I was until the London train had left. You had to be doubly careful in any case as an 'offside' split was immediately above the live rail. Luckily there was another railman on the platform next to my train and he had the presence of mind not to let the driver detach the units until I was back on the platform. I would have done the splits, with a moving train right behind me, if he had squeezed up and then set back to uncouple! As an extra precaution, when detaching units at night, a Bardic hand lamp displaying a red aspect was placed on the platform facing towards the driver of the leading unit.

Attaching and detaching units became a normal day to day occurrence when I became a leading railman working on the London platforms. There was an attachment towards the end of the morning rush hour which was known as the 'join up'. The first unit to arrive was formed of four coaches and it would stop on the twelve-car mark. The second was formed of eight coaches so the attachment took place at the eight-car mark. The mark was on the only straight piece of track adjacent to the platform and the units almost always went together on the first attempt. An extra attachment was introduced for a short while. This was formed, in the middle of the rush hour, with two four-car units, one from Seaford and one from Eastbourne. These units were attached next to the four-car mark which was situated on the sharp curve. The driver, who had been working the rear unit on one particular week, had been running 'straight on' instead of stopping six feet short and then drawing forward. This was officially classed as a collision and was frowned upon by management. On the third day, the buckeye coupling had been opened on the rear of the front unit as per usual. Both buckeyes had to be open because of the alignment of the curve. The driver, who had been lucky enough to already have an open buckeye on his unit for the first few days, ran 'straight on!' This time it was closed and there was an almighty clang as he came on a little too hard. I saw people in the front compartment jerk forward and drop back into their seats. The couplings had not connected and when the platform was clear I asked the driver to set back a little. I pulled the release chain to open the coupling. We then attempted to attach the units but soon realised that the rear coupling on the front unit had been bent out of line by the force of the impact. I got down on to the track and pulled the securing pin out of the damaged coupling. It was jammed in the raised position and would not drop to make way for the emergency screw coupling. In the end, I borrowed a sledge hammer from the permanent way department and the coupling was forcibly knocked down into the lowered position. The buffers were pulled out to the extended position and the housings were put on to the shafts to keep them in place. The screw coupling was attached to both units and the train eventually departed three quarters of an hour late. My supervisor was requested to submit a report because the driver had reported another leading railman for not opening the coupling before he called the train forward to attach. Luckily the supervisor had witnessed the incident and the leading railman was cleared of the charge. We never heard if the driver had been disciplined.

Although it never happened on the main line, the practice of going 'straight on' occasionally took place when I became a driver. In sidings, a shunter would sometimes say, 'OK to go straight on mate!' If it was dark, and you were sure that the couplings were open, you would occasionally go with it so as not to lose face. It was done gently and quietly with a quick glance to left and right to make sure that nobody was looking! It was a disciplinary matter if caught in the act by a traction inspector.

I carried out locomotive hauled coupling/uncoupling on just one occasion at Lewes. It was with an inspector's saloon and a class 33 which was more commonly known as a 'Crompton'. The train had come from Brighton and was booked to be run around in the platform loop on the branch. I donned some overalls and waited for the driver to assure me that the train heat was turned 'Off'. This was very important because the train heat jumper between the loco and saloon carried high voltage and could have caused injury if 'live' when handled. Reassured, I went in between to uncouple. The loco was then shunted on to the Brighton end for the return journey and I went in between again to reattach the coupling, jumper and pipes. The driver was on the platform lending me a bit of encouragement because it was my first time with a loco. It was a little daunting being down between two such heavy objects and the noisy loco engine above me added to the feeling of insecurity. We simultaneously decided that the coupling would go on more easily if the buffers were squeezed up a little. There was a second man on the loco who had not yet passed out for driving and he must have overheard our conversation. He squeezed the loco up tight to the saloon without any warning! Normally you could do this with someone down on the track if their back was tight up to the platform edge. On this occasion I was still standing at full height, right in between the vehicles. I dropped to the track as the driver shouted at the second man to 'STOP!' The man climbed out of the cab and watched me finish off the attachment from the platform. I climbed out from the confined space, my nerves a little flustered. The driver had patiently watched me in silence. He then turned to the slightly pale looking second man and unleashed a hurl of abuse for not asking his permission to move the loco. Suitably embarrassed, the second man climbed back in to the cab and sat down in a corner. I climbed out of my overalls as the driver apologised for the second man's haste. I learned, later on as a driver, that some kind of permission was always needed before moving a train. Even it was for just a few feet!

FLAGMAN'S DUTIES AT GLYNDE

I made quite a mistake of my own on a fine sunny morning. A flagman was required at Glynde station because the platform 'starter' signal had failed. I travelled out to begin my duties in the cab of the next available train. The sun was still out when I arrived and I was looking forward to a pleasant couple of hours in a picturesque location. The signal post phone would ring on the approach of a down train and I would pass the signalman's instructions on to the drivers. 'OK to pass this signal at danger and obey all others.' To clarify, the driver would then repeat this instruction back to me. I then held up a green flag in accordance with rule book regulations. Today this would all be done without a flagman, the driver receiving permission to pass a signal at danger via the cab radio. After an hour or so it had begun to rain very heavily. I walked back to the middle of the platform and stood under the footbridge so as to keep dry. The rain was relentless when the phone rang again and I scurried back down the platform to answer it wondering why I had volunteered for the job. The signalman gave permission for the train to 'pass at danger' and I relayed the message on to the driver. He did not react or say anything. I inquired as to whether he was going to proceed and he asked me to display a green flag. At this point I must mention that I had left the flag under the footbridge in my bag! This did not go down very well and I arrogantly told the driver that he had got permission from the signalman so what difference would a flag make? The driver was, quite understandably, incredulous and still refused to go. I was wet through by this time and I refused to walk back to get the flag for what I thought at the time was a pointless exercise. I told the driver that he was being unreasonable and making the train late. The situation seemed ridiculous and in the end I went and got the flag. The train pulled away and the driver, who was quite angry by this time, informed me that he was going to report me on arrival at Eastbourne. He kept his word and when I returned to Lewes I got a telling off from the supervisor. With hindsight, age and experience, I can see that I was wrong not to display the flag. It was, after all, a replacement for the signal. I remembered this incident later on as a driver. I would not have moved my train either if faced with similar circumstances.

SELMESTON LEVEL CROSSING

I was unlucky enough to experience another soaking in similar conditions. I had just reported to the supervisor when booking on for a night turn and he informed me that I should go on the early paper train to Selmeston. I was to manually work the automatic half barrier crossing until 6am. I would then be relieved by the early turn supervisor who was going to make his way there by car, straight from home. I carried out the normal duties of the night shift which entailed seeing out the last of the trains, cleaning the offices, waiting rooms and toilets and then sweeping the stairs, overbridge and platforms. I managed to get couple of hours rest and then went to platform 1 at about 4.30 to unload the morning papers with the junior railman. This train always consisted of a Crompton and a few parcel vans. After unloading, the papers were taken by BRUTE to the booking hall where the local newsagents would collect them, minus a couple of papers that somehow went missing each morning! The junior railman was left to move the papers by himself and I asked the driver if he would drop me off at Selmeston crossing. This was my first cab ride in a Crompton and it was quite an enjoyable and fast trip due to the light load. Having been dropped off, I proceeded to work in accordance with instructions from the signalman. It was raining hard and this was the first time that I had been to Selmeston crossing which was a rather lonely and rural spot by any standards. It was still dark when I arrived and there was no shelter whatsoever. I presumed the supervisor would be arriving soon and would probably have a comfortable time sitting in his car, listening out for the phone to ring when a train was on the approach. I can remember feeling glad that I would not be there for long! Six o'clock came and went and no relief showed up. I gave it half an hour and then phoned the signalman to ask him if he could politely ask the station supervisor to get moving. This he did but to no avail. The supervisor replied that he had no intention of sitting in the middle of nowhere in the rain! He did have a tendency to lock himself in the office and only come out in dire emergencies. I phoned a couple more times during the morning to ask for relief. I was tired, wet, unequipped with food or drink and was cold to the bone. Eventually somebody turned up at midday and the signalman kindly stopped a passenger train on the crossing to pick me up and take me back to Lewes. I arrived in a fairly grim mood and it would have made me feel better to have torn a strip off of the supervisor. He was locked in his office as per usual so I decided not to give him the satisfaction of seeing me in my dishevelled state. I went home on the first available train and eventually arrived at my front door, still soaked to the skin, at about 2pm. I had been away from home for seventeen hours so I decided to get couple of hours of sleep. I learned very a valuable lesson from this experience. Always go prepared for any eventuality. I caught the 9.00pm train back to Lewes for my next night turn. I was far too exhausted to bother with the revenge I that I had been planning for my supervisor!

THUNDERSTORM

The day had been hot and the late turn staff had seen the last of the rush hour trains away. All had gone smoothly until about 8.30pm when I noticed a light shower that was passing overhead. It did not last long but the sound of distant thunder could be heard clearly by 9pm. The sky darkened and it began to rain. The night had arrived early and soon lightning was illuminating the station on a very frequent basis. The thunder quickly became almost constant and the atmosphere was literally electric. The rain began to pour heavily and the station lights were extinguished as an enormous thunderclap exploded overhead. Looking up towards the town I could see that it was in total darkness. By this time, the night shift were arriving and I was asked to stay on and help out until the lights were back on. As luck would have it, the signals and trains were all running as normal so the next step was to acquire some Tilley lamps from the permanent way stores cupboard. We lit them quickly and began to help passengers on to the trains. Men were also stationed in the booking office and at the tops of the stairs. The supervisor was rightly concerned that no passenger should move around the station unaccompanied. Luckily it was not too busy and at times the staff outnumbered the passengers.

We remained vigilant and the storm continued unabated, the rain falling in torrents. At about 10.30pm, the signalman phoned to inform us that Cooksbridge level crossing had failed because a lightning strike had hit a relay box. This had caused a short circuit which had resulted in the barriers being automatically lowered. This was exactly what should have happened when a level crossing failed, thus keeping road traffic safe from passing trains. Unfortunately, the barriers had lowered very quickly and a car had been trapped, on the crossing, between them. Accompanied by the station master, I collected the flagging equipment bag and went to the front of the station to hire a taxi. It was only a couple of miles to Cooksbridge and the driver was asked to put his foot down.

The barriers were still down on arrival at the crossing and the car was still in situ. The rear end was against the barriers and the front end was right across the 'up' London line. Incredibly, there was a man, woman, two children and a dog still seated in the car! The signalman had put a block on both lines but these people couldn't have known that. They explained that they didn't want to stand in the rain and get wet! The station master glanced at me in sheer disbelief. We helped the family out of harm's way and then opened the barriers by pumping the gates up with manual levers. We were thanked for releasing the car and the family drove off, totally unaware of the danger that they had placed themselves in. I will never understand why these people had not moved their children to a place of safety. They had been on the crossing for about a quarter of an hour by the time we had arrived!

The station master, sensing a wetting, got back into the taxi and returned to the station. Once again, I was left to work the barriers alone and with no shelter. Cooksbridge station was tantalisingly close but I would never have heard the crossing phone above the noise of the rain and thunder. It was indeed tempting to seek shelter between trains but it was just not possible. I have always enjoyed watching a good lightning storm and this night's display was spectacular. I was however, more than a little concerned about the very high tree which was looming above me! I did not want to become another statistic of the night's events! British Rail waterproof clothing left a lot to be desired in those days but I remained at the crossing until about 1am when the last Eastbourne train passed through. A taxi was sent to collect me for the journey back to the station. The rain was beginning to ease off by this time although distant thunder could still be heard. I was cold and soaked through so I stood next to the heater in the mess room for about half an hour. The electricity was back on by this time and after a hot drink I was sent home in my third taxi of the evening. The noise and adrenalin of the evening's events kept me lying awake for quite some time before I eventually drifted off to a broken and dream filled sleep.

MOTIVE POWER AT LEWES

There was a fair selection of rolling stock which passed through the station when I worked at Lewes. Most trains were formed of CIGs, BIGs and VEPs but there was the occasional visit from a CEP 'Kent Coast' unit. The only booked workings for CEPs, as mentioned in the introduction, were the 'up' morning and 'down' evening boat trains which ran between Victoria and Newhaven Marine station. These trains were formed with eight coaches and a Motor Luggage Van. The small depot of drivers and guards from Seaford worked these trains and the morning 'up' trip was a very 'sought after' turn because it was very short. The crew travelled to Newhaven by taxi and were supposed to prep the train before departure. In reality, they could arrive just a few minutes before the train was due to leave because the Newhaven Harbour signalman would cut the units in and put the heating on in readiness for the journey. The train was then worked non-stop to Victoria. The units were berthed in sidings and the crew could go 'pass' home on the cushions. The boat train must have been one of the easiest turns on the region.

Occasionally the odd 'Thumper', 3D or 3H unit, would call at Lewes and there was also a parcels train in the afternoon which was usually worked by a Bulleid design 4 EPB unit. This would stop to deliver mail bags and Red Star parcels. Later on in the day, the unit was used for a Brighton/Seaford round trip before returning up the Brighton line to London. I had a few rides in the front of these EPB workings and the most memorable thing about them was the spacious cabs when compared with corridor stock. One hybrid unit appeared for a while and this consisted of VEP driving trailers with a

CIG motor coach and a TSO sandwiched in the centre. The days of BR blue and grey were coming to an end and liveries were varied. The CEPs were being repainted into jaffa cake 'London & South East' livery and a few CIGs followed suit. The CIGs were, however, soon painted into the new Network SouthEast red, white, blue and grey livery. Most locomotive workings were covered by BR blue class 33 and 73 locomotives.

DRIVING TRAINS

After a while I got to know a few drivers and I regularly rode to and from work in the cab. I soon learned what most of the controls were for and quite a few drivers asked me if I wanted to 'sit in the chair'. It was only a fifteen minute run between my home station and work in Lewes but this was enough to begin with. I remembered that 'dead man's handle' ache in my arm as a boy but it was great to be driving at an older age and to have a better idea of what I was actually doing. I had a few rough stops to begin with. I would apply the brake too heavily and then roll along the platform, at a slow pace, before stopping on the four-car mark. Occasionally, I would make an initial application which was too light. This would result in panic and 'coming up in a heap' at the last moment! The drivers always remained calm and never lost their nerve. It was a job which involved a lot of patience and a cool head. I discovered later that a driver could spend a lot of time waiting around for signals, departure from sidings and putting up with the innumerable kinds of delays or surprises that the railway could conjure up at a moment's notice. This could be frustrating when on your last trip of the day but you had to be pragmatic and accept that you would be late home sometimes.

I remember that my best stop was on a trip home. It was the kind of stop that stuck in your mind for a while. I was driving my first 4 BIG unit which was an unusual visitor on the Seaford branch. It was the one and only time that I had had a chance to drive with this particularly chatty driver. I can remember trying hard to concentrate and I applied about 18lb/psi to the brake when on the uphill approach to Bishopstone. I was hoping that this stop was going to be good and to my surprise the BIG unit stopped, right on the 4-car mark, as I let the brake cylinders down to 5lb/psi for a smooth stop. I had just done my first 'one application' stop. This was a total fluke but the driver was impressed and, although he was chatting, he had taken in what I had just achieved. He said, "Blimey, you've done this before!" The E.P. brake was very good and you could adjust it by using minute and precise movements of the brake handle to achieve a smooth stop. A few adjustments were usually required so a 'one application' stop tended to be a rarity.

I would usually catch the 9.00pm train when going in for a night turn. This working was on a Streatham Hill diagram and quite often the same driver would swap for this particular turn. It got him back to his home depot just in time for last orders and back then the odd pint wasn't frowned upon as it is now. In fact, he quite often let me drive so that he could finish his pint in the second man's chair! The turn was doubly lucky for him because there was time for a 'quick one' at Seaford! I had had a few drives with this man and on one particular evening I was driving at about 70mph between Newhaven and Lewes when he informed me that he was going to go to the toilet. It was dark and it was in the days before headlights so I was mortified when he just got up and went! I can remember suddenly clinging on to the controls for dear life. He did not return until I was stopping the train at Lewes and so I kept my head very low when running in to the platform. I still managed to get spotted by a mate who was finishing his late turn. He gave me a knowing smile and carried on with sweeping the platform! I must have been as white as a sheet when I booked on for duty! These were good days and I would quite often ring the bell on the way in to work so that the guard could check a few tickets.

My life then changed, very dramatically, when I met a girl and moved into a flat. I had to leave the railway because the wages were not enough for us to survive on. I landed myself a job with the Royal Mail, working as a postman. Ironically, my delivery route followed the railway line from Seaford to Bishopstone. I liked watching the trains go by but it rubbed in the fact that I missed the railway so much. I spent six years delivering letters which mostly consisted of utility bills and junk mail. I was tired of getting wet all the year round and something had to give. After some thought and re-working of the finances, I applied for the position of trainman D (trainee train driver) at Brighton depot. I managed to find the reply to my application while sorting letters one morning. I had been successful and there was a train ticket enclosed which took me to London Bridge station for a day of tests. This time it wasn't just a simple case of a quick chat with the train crew manager followed by a dozen simple mathematics questions! It was a nerve-racking day which was spent sitting in a small room with about forty other applicants. We were called into another room to do various examinations over the course of about four hours. After each exam some names were called out and these people were sent home as 'unsuccessful'. The time passed slowly and by the end of the day only three or four of us were left. The tests involved English, mathematics, logic, speed and accuracy. The last test was done on a computer; it involved pushing buttons and foot pedals whilst following a random pattern of lights on the screen. At the end of the day I had a one-to-one interview with a member of recruitment staff. Following this I had an interview with a line manager at Brighton and then a medical at Victoria. It was all nail-biting stuff but the long and short of it was that I got a position in the trainman D link at Brighton, the 'D' standing for Driver. I was owed some leave so I left the Royal Mail almost immediately.

2

Trainman D – Brighton

I was allocated a friendly traction inspector on my first day at Brighton. He was an ex-driver and he had had plenty of experience of life in the footplate grade. He set me to work learning the ropes and I became a member of the Associated Society of Locomotive Engineers and Firemen, ASLEF for short. Membership of the trade union was an absolute must when working on a job which involved so much responsibility.

Brighton was a very friendly depot. The mess room was spacious with plenty of tables and chairs and there was a television corner with sofas and a coffee table. The trainees frequented this area on breaks or when sitting spare and the older drivers had light-heartedly christened it 'the play pen'. The train crew supervisors had their own office which was adjacent to a lobby where the roster, duty and late notice cabinets were to be found. The depot had approximately one hundred drivers with about the same amount of guards so there was always someone to pass the time with if you were on a spare turn. Added to this, there were drivers from the many other depots whose crews would use the facilities: Bedford, Victoria, London Bridge, Selhurst, Norwood, Horsham, Three Bridges, Littlehampton, Bognor Regis and Eastbourne. It was good to hear how things worked at other depots and a lot of the drivers had had varied careers. It was still a time when it was easy to transfer from depot to depot so it was quite usual to meet drivers, who between them, had worked all over the UK mainland. Chatting to people in this way gave a real combined sense of knowledge and experience. It was interesting to learn how things were on different regions and also to hear drivers talking about what it was like to drive the varied types of traction which could still be found on the UK railway network at that time. The job came with deeply ingrained traditions, one of which was the passing on of knowledge as if from father to son. This 'handed down' experience was invaluable to a trainee.

As mentioned in the introduction, the trainmen Ds were used for covering guards' duties when there was a shortage. They were also utilised for working on empty stock movements and ballast duties. I was sent out route learning for a few weeks before I actually worked any trains. Guards did not get as much time on routes as drivers but they did have to know what line their train was travelling on and also the locations of station signals and

'OFF' indicators. Learning Guard's rules at the training school was fairly straightforward and most of the time was spent studying the principles of signalling and train protection. Luckily, as potential drivers, we didn't have to learn anything about tickets. We went out on a few trains to get the hang of ringing the bell and we also attended a shunting course for splitting and attaching units. This was carried out at Brighton in Montpelier Sidings while coupling wagons was covered in Three Bridges Yard. Loco coupling was learned with a pair of Cromptons at Stewart's Lane depot, Battersea. This was quite amusing because the driver who was moving one of the Cromptons thought he would have some sport with us. He pulled the loco up too short or too tight and we had to ask him very politely to adjust the distance so that we could get the screw coupling into place. This was done in jest and we were all plastered in grease by the end of the training session!

The trainman D link was mostly formed of men who were new to the job and we tended to share our experiences of what went on out on the track whilst playing pool in the mess room. There were quite a few of us and we had a lot of spare turns so that we could fill in for guards' duties at short notice. At times there could be a lot of us milling about and the older drivers, sensing some fun, would tease us and call us 'boil in the bag drivers'. We learned how to work out 'fiddles' at an early stage. You, or one of your fellow colleagues, were often allowed to get away early if you covered for one another. Fiddles were always unofficial but they got the job done and

Brighton train crew room. Situated above a modern shop, the building commands a wide view of the station and concourse. *Author*

31

somebody usually got something out of it. Members of train crew used to work fiddles out between themselves, with no intercession from the train crew supervisor. The managers knew it went on but turned a blind eye as long as everything ran smoothly. This all changed following an accident which had caused the death of a driver. The family of the rostered driver were informed of his death before any form of identification of the body had been carried out. A 'fiddle' had been worked and a different driver had been killed in the accident. From then on, a fiddle could only be carried out with the permission of the T.C.S. In this way, the whereabouts of every driver was known at all times so that a repetition of this incident could never happen.

TRAINMAN D DUTIES

The trainmen had a few specific turns of their own. These were mostly guards' duties which involved the moving of empty stock between depots. These turns were usually referred to as 'Qs' or in plain English, 'as required'. One such turn ran on Fridays only and it involved the working of '63 stock units between Lover's Walk depot and Eastleigh works. Link one drivers were utilised because they were the only men who signed the route from Farlington Junction to Bournemouth. Eastleigh works was on a diversionary route to Bournemouth so the Qs kept the drivers familiar with the route which diverged at Fareham and ran to Eastleigh via Botley. The run, in either direction, could be very quick or mind numbingly slow depending on whether the signalman placed the empties behind a Brighton/Portsmouth stopper. On arrival, we would enquire if there was a unit booked for the return journey. We would jump on the first train home if there wasn't. If there was, we would have a break in the shunters' lobby while the fitters carried out some final tests on the unit. It would be driven back and forth in a works siding so that the brakes and power circuits could be tested. This could go on for some time before the unit was signed off as 'passed' and fit for service. The entrance/exit road, which led into the works, had one of the tightest curves that I have ever seen on standard gauge track, the other being on the West Carriage road at Lover's Walk. These curves would cause the wheel flanges to scream, even at the slow speed of 5mph, the regulation speed for sidings and yards. I was sitting spare at Brighton one afternoon when a 4 BIG unit came apart as its driver pulled out of the station with a London bound train. Managers headed to the platform, expecting to see that the driver had not carried out a proper attachment between units. To their surprise, they found that the coupling had broken away between the buffet car and driving trailer. This unit had recently returned from Eastleigh works! It was a very unusual incident and it was pure luck that it hadn't happened on the main line!

We had a Qs turn between Lover's Walk and Fratton depots for a short time. This was also used for moving stock which required maintenance attention. A more regular duty was to run empties up to Redhill where we would be relieved by South Eastern men who would take the units on to Ashford's Chart Leacon depot. The 'Selhurst Qs' was the most frequently worked of the empty stock turns. This moved units between Brighton and Selhurst which were the South Central's biggest depots. The trainmen had very little to do on these duties. Brake tests were carried out when required and occasionally a train would have to be seen away from a platform if stopped on a signal. There could be a lot of waiting around at Selhurst if a unit was booked to run on the return trip. If this working ran 'as booked' it would leave Selhurst and run right up to London Bridge where it would be boxed in by a suburban unit for quite some time. If there was a good signal-man on the panel at Three Bridges you could come out of the yard and change ends at Norwood Junction. This could save a lot of time. I remember a link two driver once asking me if I would take the return unit back to Brighton on my own as he 'had to be somewhere!' I had not long signed the route for guarding and Selhurst was quite a complicated yard. I had done quite a bit of driving on these Qs turns but I was not ready to be put 'up the front' on my own as I had only been out on the track for a few months! The driver understood when I turned him down but I'm quite sure he would have gone through with it if I had agreed! There was a converted CEP unit which was based at Selhurst and I once worked this, as a guard, on an empty stock move to Brighton. It had been renumbered as 930 082 and had been rebuilt as a three-car route learning unit. I would love to have had a drive but my driver hadn't worked any CEP stock for a while. To my disappointment he used the exercise as a refresher course! The theatre style seating and large amount of windscreen did however give a superb view of the road ahead.

There was a rather dreaded nightshift which a crew would, sometimes unsuspectingly, get landed with on the 21.00 spare turn. Lover's Walk had one or two class 09 '350s' which would occasionally have to be taken up to Norwood Yard for re-fuelling. This was an arduous task which usually took a couple of hours in each direction. 27mph was the maximum speed that these locomotives could attain! The trip would start late in the night, so as not to get in the way of any other services. The 350s gave a hard ride and the eighty mile round trip to Norwood was quite a lesson in patience! Norwood depot was quite small compared to its much larger neighbour of Selhurst and an hour's quiet was much needed while the loco was serviced. There wasn't much for the trainman to do and he was only present to carry out rear end protection, should a mishap occur.

One other turn involved moving wagons between Three Bridges and Redhill yards. The trainman worked as second man on Cromptons or class 73 Electro-diesels which were commonly referred to as E.Ds. The trains were usually brought into Redhill from the Tunbridge line where we would relieve the crew because the South Eastern men did not sign the route down to

Three Bridges. It was a rather short run for we Brighton men but it did keep some diesel work for the top link drivers.

Life was not too exciting for trainmen when working as a guard on passenger trains. There were no ticket duties so a lot of time was spent in the guard's van, only coming out when the train needed seeing away from a station. There were many Thameslink turns which were worked with class 319 units. These services only required a guard between Brighton and Gatwick as driver only operation (D.O.O.) was not permitted south of the airport. It was not unusual to guard on three or four return trips in a day. I did learn one important thing when working passenger trains as a guard. I would not have chosen it as a career for all of the tea in China! Guards took the brunt of passenger complaints if things were not running to plan and the stress very often showed on their faces. Luckily, 319s were worked from the rear or intermediate cab and at least offered somewhere to be out of the limelight!

I made a mistake on one occasion when guarding on a Hastings to Brighton service. The train had stopped at Cooden Beach station and I had not noticed that the platform starter signal was at danger. I gave the driver 'two on the bell' but he was on the ball and did not pull away. I found this lack of concentration on the guard's part extremely irritating when I eventually became a driver myself. This would sometimes occur if the guard was busy with tickets or had somebody asking questions as they were carrying out platform duties. Occasionally, a driver would get caught out by this and it would result in disciplinary proceedings. The driver's reminder appliance (DRA) was fitted to all units soon after I began driving. It was a very effective way of eliminating human error. The driver could not pull away against a danger signal because the DRA cut the power to the traction motors while displaying a bright red light in the cab. It was manually operated and it soon became an automatic reflex to use it when in this situation. We were also taught to put the brake handle in the full service position at the same time. Luckily, the driver did not hold the Cooden Beach incident against me and it was soon forgotten.

I was sitting spare later on in the year. It was cold and there had been quite a layer of snow overnight. I knew that I would not be left to sit around for too long because units were failing due to the icy conditions. Sure enough, a passenger train failed at Plumpton soon after I had got comfortable. I was sent, with a driver, to collect an empty unit from Lover's Walk. We were to make a rescue attempt on the failed unit and so we headed up the main line to Wivelsfield where we changed ends. We then ran back down through Keymer Junction and on to the Eastbourne line. We were stopped on the signal before Plumpton station and were instructed to pass it at danger due to the line being occupied by the failed unit. The rear end of this unit should have been protected by three detonators placed twenty yards apart and three hundred yards to the rear. This regulation was in place so that the driver of an assisting unit would receive an audible warning on approach to a failed unit. The guard of the failed unit was supposed to meet the assisting train on its approach to the detonators. He was then supposed to guide the assisting driver in on foot while giving clear verbal instructions as to the failed train's whereabouts. No detonators had been placed on the track and there was no sign of the guard. We slowly made our way forward and spied the failed train waiting in the platform ahead.

The guard was holding up a red flag and was standing next to the rear of the failed unit! He had placed three detonators, two inches apart, at about twelve feet from the back of his train! My driver was a little cross at this incompetence and he slid the cab window open and asked the guard a perfectly reasonable question. "What are you trying to do, blow my *******
wheel off?" The guard clearly did not have a clue about the rules concerning train 'protection' and although not reported for his lack of competence, he did lose his job a month or so later because he was involved in a similar incident. A train that he was working on had come apart between units. This was a rare occurrence and when asked if he had carried out a proper brake test he replied that he had. He was asked to describe the procedure and it was soon realised that he had absolutely no idea of how to do it! Incredibly, two other units had failed between Plumpton and Lewes earlier on the same day. A de-icing unit had failed when assisting another a de-icing unit which had broken down! The thinnest amount of ice could cause problems with the conductor rail and I never did understand why diesel units were not employed on de-icing duties.

The de-icing units were mostly worked by link one drivers and they were popular duties because they made a change from racing around on passenger trains. These units were also fitted with equipment for laying sandite in the leaf fall season. I worked a few guarding diagrams on the Chipman's weed killer train in the summer time. This was quite an experience and was the only time that I got to ride in the cab of class 20s. They were quite strange when compared to our usual locomotives but the cabs were more comfortable than the dingy guard's compartment on the weed killing coaches.

Working with locomotives on ballast duties brought a welcome break from guarding on passenger trains. Due to engineering works, most ballast turns ran on Sundays or overnight during the week. A great deal of time could be spent waiting around for the site manager's instructions. You could wait for a few hours and then get a call for the train to be moved just a couple of feet. Other jobs would involve constant instructions and many movements. Diversions could sometimes be had if it was quiet. I remember showing my driver the Hale-Bopp comet one night when we were waiting between Hassocks and Clayton tunnel. He hadn't been aware that there was a comet so it passed some time and gave us a break from the vibration of the class

37's engine. The 37s were phased in on the Southern for ballast work because the Cromptons were becoming life expired. The examples that were coming through were, in my opinion, in much worse condition than the Cromptons. I remember spending half an hour watching my driver trying to coax a 37 out of Chichester yard on wet rails with a loaded spoil train. He got there in the end but it was painful to watch and the language was colourful! The cab heaters always seemed to do the opposite of what was needed and were often broken in the winter. I once spent six miserable hours at Stone Cross while laying ballast on a Sunday morning. The heating was jammed on and we couldn't get out of the cab because there were constant calls for us to move up and down the line. I always found the 37s rather uncomfortable. The Cromptons' cabs were spacious and had nice seats with plenty of leg room so it was always a bonus to find one on your train. I was sitting in the cab of a Crompton at Stoat's Nest Junction when news came through on the radio of the death of Princess Diana. My driver and I had been dozing but this news brought us to our senses quickly. It had been passed on to us from an excitable permanent way man who had been sitting next to the line in his van. We had had a bit of a night. At one point we had had to set back into the siding at Reedham, the site manager waving us back from the far end of the train. We had a fair few wagons on and he must have lost concentration because the buffers at the end of the siding did the braking for us! No damage had been done but my driver mentioned a few choice words when the site manager apologised over the radio. To finish the night off, our taxi back to Brighton was delayed by an hour or more so sleep was most welcome when it eventually came.

I can remember a hair-raising run with a very shabby looking class 37. We were hauling a heavy load of ballast spoil between Littlehampton and Three Bridges yard and were booked to run via the Mid-Sussex line. Those familiar with the line will know that there are a lot of gradients encountered as it winds its way along the Arun Valley towards Horsham. For some unexplained reason, the signalmen on this Sunday were a little on the slow side with giving us the road through each section. The poor 37 did not appreciate all of the standing starts that the signalmen were dishing out to it and before long the fire bell was ringing in number one cab because the engine was starting to overheat. My driver was quite a character. He always wore a smile and never seemed to be fazed by anything, fire alarms included. We ran the last half of the journey to 'Bridges' with a rag stuffed between the clapper and bell! I enquired as to whether I should look back out of the side window to see if there was any smoke coming from the engine room. My driver replied "No. You never saw or heard a thing. There's a match on this afternoon and this pile of **** will get us there if I have to push it myself!" It was then made clear that we were not risking sitting around for hours to wait for another loco to come and assist us. We made it into the yard a little late and

I was glad to walk away from the 37 without so much as a singed eyebrow. We looked into the engine room on arrival and all seemed to be well. It was a little on the warm side and in hindsight I think that the train should have been double-headed from the outset. The engine had been severely overworked and I have to admire the fact that it had survived the run under such circumstances.

We would very often collect a ready prepared train from Three Bridges yard. I would give the driver a brake test and then have a walk around to check that all was well. The reception road signal would clear and we would gently pull out of the yard and head on to the main line in the direction of our place of work. I was lucky enough to drive a 37 from the yard down to Arundel Junction via Hove and I must say that it was a very different experience from driving an EMU. The train was very heavy with ballast hoppers and it took some careful handling. Eyes were always on the ammeters when taking power and you certainly had to be patient when trying to achieve something near to the line speed. The train brake was very snatchy when compared to the smooth and easily adjustable electro-pneumatic brake of '63 stock. These locomotives could be quick off the mark when pulling away 'light' but they were way behind the class 73 electro-diesels, especially when they were in contact with the conductor rail.

The electro-diesels had comfortable cabs and could certainly put up a lively performance when hauling a passenger train. I once attended a training course in London, after which, the instructor took six of us for a ride on a Victoria to Gatwick Airport 'Gatwick Express' service. The E.D's cab was 'full and standing' and the ride was incredible at 90mph. We were thrown all over the place at Earlswood Junction which was taken at the full line speed of 80mph! These locos could be a little sluggish when running 'off the juice' due to the very low-powered diesel engine which took over when there was no conductor rail. I worked quite a few turns as second man on these locos, particularly on the Redhill/Three Bridges wagon movements. I can remember working on an E.D. in the London Bridge area. We had a long load of spoil wagons and on approach to the 'Bridge' we were signalled on to the South Eastern through lines. My driver was OK with this because he worked the Thameslink services which utilised these lines but I hadn't signed the Eastern side so it was a bit of a learning curve when it came to doing a runround in the platform. There was quite a gradient, and having uncoupled, I made sure that the wagons were firmly secured with a few handbrakes. We then proceeded towards Blackfriars, all the while looking out for the shunt signal which would take us back through the station, via another platform. My driver spotted it and stopped the engine. He had been on the footplate for many years but had never carried out a shunt on the Eastern side of London Bridge. The lines were busy and the complicated track layout made it not the easiest of places to go signal spotting! Relying on your wits and the wits of your driver was a good way to gain experience and it did instil a kind of sixth sense when looking out for hazards and useful markers. We managed the run-round and I hooked the wagons back on to the locomotive in front of a large and curious audience. I can't imagine that this kind of entertainment was provided too often at London Bridge!

This same driver relished night ballast work because you could sometimes get your head down for a few hours. On one occasion we worked overnight with a Crompton on the London Road viaduct. We were regularly asked to move up for a short distance at a time and I was amazed to see this driver fall asleep, with his chin down on his chest, within seconds of applying the brake when asked to stop. This was an example of how many years of experience and familiarity with the job made for a good driver. It took a cool and relaxed head to be so sure of yourself when in the midst of such noise and chaos.

The worst turn that I ever worked on a ballast duty was in the Quarry tunnel, which is situated deep under the North Downs. We had to work in the wrong direction on the down road because the up road was being re-laid. My driver was not the most talkative of fellows and we spent seven gloomy hours, halfway along the length of the tunnel. The windows had to be closed at all times because of the noise and dust. The E.D's engine needed to be kept running because we had to make small movements. The air in the cab was hot and stifling! The engineers had put some ventilation equipment in the tunnel but it was pretty uncomfortable when you had to get out and walk to a refuge for the call of nature! The air was thick with fumes from the engine and must have been very unpleasant for the workmen. This duty seemed to go on forever and it was a huge relief when we got out of the tunnel and back into daylight. It had been a beautiful sunny day outside and I cannot imagine what it must have been like for the men who originally constructed this 1 mile 353yard-long tunnel.

The training school

I spent approximately eighteen months guarding trains, at the roster clerk's mercy, before being sent to Croydon for the driver's rules and traction courses. The rules and theory part of the traction course took place at the Network South Central Training Centre which was located just down the road from East Croydon station. We also went out on 'static days' to look around the actual units.

DRIVER'S RULES
'Driver's rules' was quite a long course and I have not covered it in great detail here because the subject would require an entire volume of its own. The course was carried out using the older version of the rule book. This book was subsequently replaced due to its unintelligible nature. According to the Brighton traction inspectors, copies had been sent to some top university professors for examination and the verdict came back that the book made no sense at all! The updated version arrived in full Technicolor and was written in plainer English. The driver's rules included technical information regarding 'train protection' and 'passing signals at danger'. There were fifteen different reasons why a signal could be passed in this way, should the need arise. It was pretty heavy going but at the same time quite interesting. All manner of disastrous scenarios were thrown at us and we were asked to explain how we would protect lines, trains and passengers from the worst imaginable nightmare! Now and then, when things got complicated, the canteen and smoking room became more of a draw. The subsidised meals were of good quality and I was told off twice by the instructor for dozing off with a full belly! I took my driver's rules exam just after lunch on a Friday afternoon. The exam was oral and my examiner made a point of letting me know that he could tell whether I would pass or fail within five minutes of starting! He was an old school traction inspector from Selhurst depot and after an hour or two he said he was "off to the pub" and signed me off as 'passed'. A couple of men on our course failed rules and had to re-take the exam after being given more time to revise. I returned to Brighton and collected a much coveted driver's bag from the train crew supervisor. Carrying the bag was a way of earning a bit of status in a job where seniority and experience was still very much ingrained into the men.

SHORT CIRCUITING BAR/HOOK SWITCH POLE TRAINING

The class of about twelve trainmen were sent to Waterloo for short-circuiting bar training shortly after completion of the rules course. This instrument was used for short circuiting the conductor rail when in an emergency situation. Our initiation with 'the bar' was carried out on a siding to the east of the station and it was fair to say that nobody was really looking forward to practising on a live conductor rail. I'm sure that we were all expecting a huge flash and bang when the bar was put in place! The instructor demonstrated the procedure and then we were all given a turn at cleaning the bottom of the conductor rail with a wooden paddle, to remove grease and dirt. This was to ensure good electrical contact between all points. The bar was then jerked into place quickly so as to create a short circuit between the conductor rail and running rail. As it turned out, it was rather disappointing as far as the fireworks were concerned. The most that I heard was a short buzz when someone applied the bar a little too slowly. We were also taught how to use a hook switch pole. Hook switches were located at strategic locations on the conductor rail and the pole was used to open them should a local current isolation be required. A pole was carried in each driving cab and was more commonly used for picking up items that were dropped under trains by passengers! We also went to Raynes Park electrical control room to see how the conductor rail was monitored by technicians. The interior was not dissimilar to a modern signal box and one of the staff gave us a talk on the workings of the room. The staff would try to restore the current only fifteen seconds after spotting a fault or unexplained isolation. They would make four attempts in all before trying to find out the cause of the problem. This was done because the conductor rail could often be momentarily shorted out by small objects which fell on to the track for whatever reason.

1963 STOCK 'TRACTION' COURSE

Having finished driver's rules, we were sent to Croydon to complete the 1963 stock (400 series) traction course. The 4 CIG (class 421) and 4 BIG (class 422) units were designed in 1963 and were constructed at York. They entered service between 1964 and 1972 and were introduced to replace the life expired pre-war express stock which consisted of 6 PAN, 6 PUL, 4 COR, 4 RES and 4 BUF units. The 4 VEPs (class 423) were constructed at York and Derby and were introduced between 1967 and 1974. These units replaced the pre-war 4 LAVs, 2 BILs and 2 HALs. Although they were originally constructed to be used on semi-fast and stopping service diagrams, the VEPs were frequently utilised on express workings. Various refurbishments were carried out on many 400 series units over the years and this resulted in the appearance of various sub-classes. The VEPs had their brake vans shortened to make room for an extra passenger compartment and some were temporarily converted for use on Gatwick Airport to London Victoria 'Rapid City

Link' workings. Eleven 4 BIGs were later converted into 3 COP (Corridor Open Plan) units. The buffet cars were removed and, to aid passenger security, the seating plan was opened out and the compartments were dispensed with. These units were intended for use on the Coastway services but occasionally saw use on the Brighton main line. Some 4 VEP units were converted for the same reasons. They were classified 4 VOP (Vestibule Open Plan). All '63 stock units were replaced by class 375/377 units by the end of 2005.

The driving cab ends were formed of steel reinforced fibreglass and all coaches were based on the standard Mk 1 design. Each four-car unit measured 265ft and weighed in at approximately 151 tonnes. The formation consisted of two driving trailer composites (DTC), one motor brake second (MBS) and one trailer second (TS). The 4 BIG units had a trailer buffet (TB) in place of the trailer second. These vehicles were fitted with a separate motor generator which, when turned on the by the buffet steward, supplied power to the kitchen facilities. Extra batteries were also carried and these were fitted with an isolation switch which could be operated by the driver in the event of a fire on the vehicle.

There seems to be some doubt as to the origin of the Southern Region 'CIG' multiple unit code. 'IG' was the telegraphic code for Brighton in the days of the London, Brighton and South Coast Railway. My 1963 stock traction manual states that CIG stands for 'Corridor Intermediate Guard' which certainly makes sense as it describes the units in typical Southern style. The 'B' in BIG stood for buffet. VEP stood for 'Vestibule Electro-Pneumatic brake'.

The traction course was far more interesting than the driver's rules but mechanical and electrical knowledge of the units brought even more complicated rules into the equation. These would cover scenarios such as brake faults or mechanical/electrical failures. We were taught how to assist or be assisted by other units in the event of a total failure. Sometimes a dead unit could still be driven if attached to an assisting unit because each was fitted with 'select back' circuitry. This allowed control power to be taken from the assisting unit if the 27-pin jumper cables were connected. Care did have to be taken, so as not to transfer a fault across to the assisting unit. The workings of the units were explained by following schematic diagrams and stacks of photocopied handouts. The theory was reinforced by a couple of trips each week to Streatham Hill down sidings where we learned to carry out brake tests and how to prepare units for service (see Appendix). On each visit, we would walk around our unit and identify all of the exterior, interior and underside equipment. Although repetitive, this practice taught us to locate things quickly and everything was examined in detail with enthusiastic explanations from the instructors (see chapters 4, 5, 6 and 7). We also learned how to attach and detach units as a driver. One of the men on the course had never driven a train before and he carried out his first attachment by throwing the power handle straight into notch four (weak field). There was a surge of power and then a jolting crunch as the units came together. Luckily there was no damage done although the poor trainee suffered a bit of ribbing from the rest of us. Our instructor found the whole episode quite amusing and attaching/detaching units 'nicely' was certainly harder than the instructors, who were all ex-drivers, made it look!

Occasionally, an older chap came to instruct us on the static days. This man was a 'no-nonsense' Londoner and he did not take prisoners when it came to dealing with faults on units. He would have made a perfect sergeant major in the army and I believe that we learned lessons through fear more than anything else! He was very knowledgeable and in his spare time he carried out driving exams for steam engine drivers on preserved railways. He would disable the unit by isolating air cocks and miniature circuit breakers. He would then give you ten minutes to sort out the mess and get the unit running. As the time ran out he would harass you until you fixed the problem or got into such a confused state that he would pick someone else to show you how it was done. On one particular day, he made up an imaginary scenario which involved a twelve-car train that had failed on the Ouse Valley viaduct. He selected his target and proceeded with what was to become a nightmare situation for any train driver. He destroyed any suggestion of a way that the train could be got moving and the poor trainee got into a real muddle. At one point he sent the imaginary guard back to protect the rear of the train while the driver looked for the fault. The instructor came back with "No, the guard just moved here and doesn't speak a word of ******* English!" Things went from bad to worse and by the end of the grilling it was dark and foggy, raining and windy, and one unit had caught fire with passengers getting out on to the viaduct to escape the flames! The poor trainman was physically shaking with nerves by the end of this treatment. It was no fun to watch this, especially when you knew that you could be the next man to be put on the spot. No harm was meant but it did show us that we really could be put to the test when out driving on our own. When the course had finished we were each given a date for the traction examination and it did nothing to encourage us when we found out that it was the 'sergeant major' who was taking the exams. They were to be held at Streatham Hill on a 'one person per day' basis. My exam was booked for the Friday and it followed the failure of all four Monday to Thursday men!

The exam day arrived and I made my way to Streatham Hill with deep foreboding. We made our way to the carriage shed and the examiner asked if I would mind an observer tagging along. I did not like to refuse and as it turned out, he was a friendly old railwayman who did his best to put me at ease whenever possible. The morning was spent looking at the electrical equipment on a 4 CIG unit. Most of the test was verbal and to my astonishment the examiner gave me some prompts when I got stuck on a few things. He produced some chalk from his pocket and drew out a few circuit diagrams on the side of the unit. When lunchtime came I was given two options. I could look at my books to study the braking system in readiness for the afternoon or I could go with the examiner and his follower to the café outside the station. I chose the café and said, "If I don't know the brakes by now I won't know them in half an hour's time!" The truth was that I was mentally exhausted and just needed a break. We had a hot drink and made small talk before going to the down sidings to resume the exam. Things went fairly smoothly and after about two hours we climbed up into a cab. The examiner said, "You've done really well so far today. I have one more question and then you can go home!" I thanked heaven that it was nearly over and I thought that maybe I had misjudged my examiner. He was turning out to be fairer than I had given him credit for.

I was asked to imagine that I was on a faulty unit which had had the brakes isolated on the front coach. The unit had an electric parking brake which meant that there was no handbrake in the driving cab. The parking brake was back on the motor coach on these units. What would I do before moving the train? My mind went totally blank and in sheer panic I came out with a succession of very lame answers. I was informed that I had done well so far but I was now on my last chance to answer the question correctly or I would fail the exam! I went very quiet and there was a long awkward silence. I do not know where the answer came from but I suddenly blurted it out. "Before it could be moved, the affected unit would need assistance from another unit on the front to 'box in' the affected coach. The passengers would have to be de-trained!" The examiner gave me a serious look and then smiled and said, "You've passed, but every time I see you I am going to ask you the same question. I think that you will never forget the answer." I agreed! We parted and I returned to Brighton with a huge weight off my mind. I never saw this man again but he was right, I never forgot the answer to that question!

ROUTES AND C.S.R. COURSE

The traction exam was followed by two short training courses. The first was a one-day course which involved being trained in the operation of the cab secure radio (C.S.R.) The radio allowed direct communication between the driver and signalmen at all times without having to stop a train at a signal post telephone. It was set up by punching in the relevant area code and signal number from which a train was beginning its journey. The signalman would then send the train identification number to the radio set. If this corresponded with the number on the driver's duty sheet it proved that the driver was working on the correct train.

The second course provided a brief introduction to route learning. We

4 CIG 1904 (Originally built as 7332) is seen on the down slow line at Stoat's Nest Junction on 9th July 1997 whilst working a semi-fast service from Victoria to Brighton during the period when the Connex livery was replacing that of Network SouthEast. *Chris Evans*

spent a couple of hours covering the theory in a classroom at Crawley and this was followed by some practical examination of an actual route. We were sent out in pairs to gather as much information as possible about a route of which none of us had any previous knowledge. The Purley to Caterham branch was selected and we spent the rest of the day in the cabs of class 455 units, making notes and asking the drivers questions about speed restrictions, junctions and braking marks for stations, etc. The second day was spent drawing up a detailed map of the route in the classroom.

The driving cab and driving trailer equipment

This chapter contains details of the driving cab and underframe equipment to be found on the two driving trailer composite coaches that were formed on each end of a 1963 unit. The following chapter contains an explanation of the equipment which was to be found on the motor brake second coach. I have not included a chapter on the trailer seconds/buffets because these vehicles carried no traction or driving equipment. The underframe on all coaches carried: an auxiliary reservoir, a brake chest which contained a triple valve (see chapter 6), a triple valve isolating cock (T.V.I.C.), an E.P. brake isolating cock (E.P.I.C.) and a brake cylinder release cord. Brake pipe and main reservoir isolating cocks, commonly known as angle cocks, were to be found on all coach ends within a unit. The DTCs were fitted with bogie brake isolating cocks, one per bogie. These isolating cocks were only operated in exceptional circumstances such as a failure of equipment or when a unit had to be driven, with a brake fault, to the nearest depot for repair.

Phase one CIG driving cab from unit 1750 (originally built as unit 7305). The phase one units were fitted with 'tram' style power handles. The driver's reminder appliance is set and the brake handle is in the full service position. *Jamie Little*

Phase two CIG cab from unit 1805 (originally built as unit 7432). The phase two units were fitted with the later style of power handle. The driver's reminder appliance is not set and the brake handle is in the full service position. Note: the E.P. key is in the separate master switch/reverser. *Ashley Barton*

POWER HANDLE AND DRIVER'S SAFETY DEVICE (D.S.D.)

The power handle, also known as the dead man's handle, was combined with the driver's safety device. It had to be held down at all times when the master switch was in the forward or reverse positions. The emergency brake would be applied and power to the traction motors would be cut if the driver let go of the handle for whatever reason. The power handle had to be returned to the 'off' position to reset the driver's safety device. The master switch could only be operated if unlocked with a master/E.P. key (see chapter 8). When turned 'on', it supplied a 70v feed to the electro-pneumatic brake, compressor control wire, automatic warning system and power handle. It operated a pilot valve which fed main reservoir air to the automatic warning system and it opened an isolating valve which charged the brake pipe, also from the main reservoir.

There were two distinct types of power handle. The phase one units were fitted with 'tram' style handles which incorporated the master switch and reverser. Handles on the phase two units had a separate master switch/reverser. Each type had four power positions or 'notches' (see chapter 7). These would group the motors into series or parallel circuits until weak field was reached in the highest notch. In theory, the driver could place the power handle straight to the highest notch because the system was controlled by a camshaft which applied power to the motors at a measured rate. In reality, this practice would speed up the camshaft which could sometimes cause an electrical overload. In normal practice, each notch was taken for a few moments before moving up to the next. Acceleration would continue while the tractive effort exceeded the resistance of the train to movement. The unit would run at its 'balancing speed' when these two factors evened out. All '63 units had a maximum permitted running speed of 90mph. The South Western division fitted some 4 CIG units with an extra stage of field weakening which allowed for a higher rate of acceleration. These units quickly became known as 'Greyhounds' and, when on test, reached speeds in excess of 100mph.

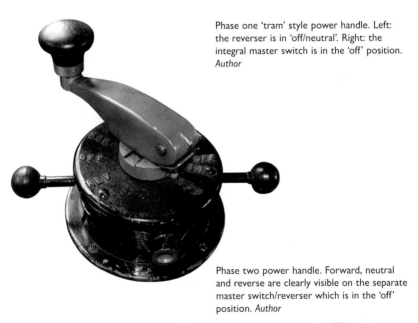

Phase one 'tram' style power handle. Left: the reverser is in 'off/neutral'. Right: the integral master switch is in the 'off' position. *Author*

Phase two power handle. Forward, neutral and reverse are clearly visible on the separate master switch/reverser which is in the 'off' position. *Author*

SERIES ONLY SWITCH

The series only switch was located on the extreme right hand side of the dashboard. It was designed to notch resistors out of circuit quickly in order to gain high acceleration when pulling away towards a steep rising gradient, such as that which led out of Folkestone Harbour. Once selected, the power handle would have been placed directly to the weak field position. Full series would then be reached very quickly but the power would not progress beyond this.

CONTROL CIRCUIT GOVERNOR

Each unit was fitted with a fail-safe device known as a 'control circuit governor'. This was incorporated into the braking system to prevent power being applied if there was not sufficient brake force available to stop the unit. A 'click' could be heard in the driving cab when the C.C.G. reinstated the control circuit as the brake pipe became fully charged. The power handle would not operate until this process had been completed.

THREE POSITION BRAKE HANDLE

The three position brake handle was used to apply the self-lapping 'application and release' electro-pneumatic brake and the self-lapping 'application only' Westinghouse automatic air brake. The brake handle positions were 'release', 'full service' and 'emergency' (see chapter 7 for diagram). The handle vented the brake pipe to '0' when placed in the 'emergency' position. This position also charged the main reservoir pipe. The 'release' position allowed the main reservoir pipe to charge the brake pipe quickly. The handle was fitted with a release prevention device which stopped the brake pipe from being charged until it was brought fully back to the 'release' position.

BRAKE SELECTOR SWITCH

This switch allowed the driver to select between the electro-pneumatic or Westinghouse automatic air brakes. Note: the automatic brake would take over if the E.P. brake failed when making an application. If this happened there would be a momentary loss of brake so the automatic brake would compensate by applying a little extra air to the brake cylinders.

BRAKE GAUGES AND SPEEDOMETER

From left to right were the 'Duplex' gauge which displayed the brake pipe and main reservoir pressures in pounds per square inch, the brake cylinder gauge which displayed the amount of brake which was being applied, also in pounds per square inch, and the speedometer which measured speed in miles per hour only.

Brake gauges from 4 CIG unit 1805. The 'Duplex' gauge (left) is displaying that the brake pipe is fully charged at 70lb/psi and the main reservoir is charged at 100lb/psi. The brake cylinder reads 50lb/psi displaying that the brake handle is in the full service position. *Ashley Barton*

AUTOMATIC WARNING SYSTEM (A.W.S.)/ TRAIN PROTECTION AND WARNING SYSTEM (T.P.W.S.) RESET BUTTON AND SUNFLOWER INDICATOR

The automatic warning system/train protection and warning system reset button was located below the sunflower indicator. The brake would make an emergency application if the driver did not react to the A.W.S. warning horn within a few seconds. To cancel the warning the reset button had to be depressed and then released. The sunflower indicator displayed black on a clear signal and black and yellow on a cautionary or danger signal. The A.W.S. could be isolated by turning a sealed handle which was positioned near to the top right hand side of the driver's windscreen. A unit could not be taken into service if the A.W.S. had been isolated or if the seal was broken or missing.

TRAIN PROTECTION AND WARNING SYSTEM (T.P.W.S.) DISPLAY PANEL AND ISOLATION SWITCHES

The train protection and warning system worked in conjunction with the A.W.S. The display panel was situated above the driver's windscreen on the right hand side.

The panel contained a red 'brake demand' light which, if flashing, meant the T.P.W.S. had initiated an emergency brake application which the driver had not yet acknowledged. The light was steady when the T.P.W.S. had initiated an emergency brake application which the driver had acknowledged.

There was a yellow 'temporary isolation/fault' light which, if flashing, meant a fault had been detected with the T.P.W.S. equipment. The light was steady when a temporary isolation had been initiated.

The yellow 'train stop override' button was used to disable the 'brake demand' for short periods, such as when a driver was instructed to pass a T.P.W.S. fitted signal at danger.

There was a temporary isolation switch which was used to disable the brake demand when driving under certain operational conditions such as when propelling a unit or driving during temporary block working. There was also a T.P.W.S. isolation switch which was located in a sealed box on top of the handbrake equipment. A unit could not be taken into service if the T.P.W.S. had been isolated or if the seal was broken or missing.

D.R.A. DRIVER'S REMINDER APPLIANCE
This switch was operated when stationary at a danger signal. The button illuminated red and disabled the power handle when pushed 'in'. If faulty, a glass seal had to be broken before the device could be isolated.

CAB SECURE RADIO
The cab secure radio was mounted on the right hand side of the cab. It was fitted with a telephone style handset and displayed the train identification number on a digital screen. In an emergency, the signalmen could speak to all drivers in a selected area at the same time. This facility was sometimes used to stop all trains in that area. In this instance the radio's screen would display 'STOP'. There was also an emergency button for the driver to use. This would give call priority if the signalman had more than one incoming call.

HORN VALVE
The two-tone air horns were mounted on the driving cab roof. They were used in compliance with the rule book such as when carrying out shunting moves and entering or exiting tunnels.

DASHBOARD AND HEADLIGHT TOGGLE SWITCHES
These switches were located on the left hand side of the dashboard and allowed the driver to select the foot rest heater, demister, meter lights (all gauges were illuminated in red), cab lights and route indicator lights. There was a separate toggle switch for the headlight.

INDICATOR FLAGS
The indicator flags were located on the right hand side of the dashboard and read as follows:
E.P; 'ON': electro-pneumatic brake selected.
Line; 'ON': unit in contact with the conductor rail.
M.G; 'ON': 70v supply available from the motor generator.
Earth fault; 'NORM' no earth fault, 'TRIP' earth fault miniature circuit breaker tripped.

EP (BRAKE SUPPLY) WILL
SHOW 'ON' ONLY IF
SELECTOR SWITCH IS IN
EP. 'OFF' IN AUTO.

DASHBOARD BUTTONS

These buttons were located on the right hand side of the dashboard. The engine stop button was located below the speedometer on phase one units.

Overload reset; each unit was fitted with a traction motor overload device. The device would cut the power to the traction motors if they drew current to an excessively high peak. The overload reset button had to be pressed for approximately five seconds to reinstate the circuit. It could only be used when the power handle was in the 'off' position. The button could also be used to start the diesel engine on a KB class 33/1 locomotive if coupled in multiple.

Aux. power 'on'; this button was used to start the diesel engine on a class 73 locomotive or to switch a motor luggage van on to battery conditions if coupled in multiple.

Aux. power 'off'; this button was used to stop the diesel engine and lower the shoes on a class 73 locomotive. It was also used to return a motor luggage van to line conditions.

Engine stop; this button was used to stop the engine on a KB class 33/1 locomotive if coupled in multiple.

Note: If the aux power and engine stop buttons were depressed it would affect the compressor control wire and would stop the compressors running. It would also affect the run back of the camshaft.

EXHAUSTER SPEED UP/BRAKE RELEASE BUTTON

This button was used to speed up the exhauster of an assisting motor luggage van or locomotive when working a vacuum braked train.

MINIATURE CIRCUIT BREAKERS (MCBs)

The driving cab miniature circuit breakers were located on the bulkhead behind the driver's head.

Miniature circuit breakers, 1963 stock driving cab. M.C.B.s highlighted in yellow were on the driving trailer auxiliary circuit. Those highlighted in green were on the control supply circuit. *Author's collection*

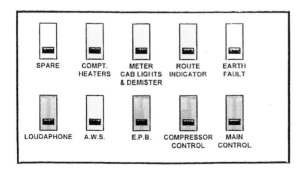

LOUDAPHONE (CAB TO CAB / BRAKE VAN COMMUNICATION EQUIPMENT)

Loudaphones were fitted in each driving cab and brake van. They were used for contact between the driver and guard. There was a 'call' button which sounded a buzzer and a 'speak' button which had to be depressed when the mouth piece was spoken in to.

PADDLES X 2, SHOE FUSE SPANNER X 1, SHORT-CIRCUITING BAR X 1 AND HOOK SWITCH POLE X 1 (PER CAB)

These tools were mounted in a recess on the bulkhead behind the second man's seat. Placing a wooden paddle between each collector shoe and the conductor rail would isolate a unit from the 750v dc supply. This procedure would sometimes be carried out if a shoe fuse needed changing. The shoe fuse spanner was used for changing shoe/ribbon fuses. Paddles were commonly displayed in cab windows to inform other drivers that the handbrake had been applied at that end. A paddle could also be jammed between the driver's cab cubicle door and the corridor connection. This would stop the door vibrating loudly when in service. The short-circuiting bar and hook switch pole were used to make emergency current isolations. (See 'Short-circuiting bar/hook switch pole training.)

Wooden paddle. Two 'paddles' were carried in each driving cab. *Author*

RED FLAG, TRACK CIRCUIT OPERATING CLIPS AND DETONATORS

These tools were housed on the bulkhead, above and behind the driver's head. They were used for 'train protection' in emergencies such as train failure or derailment.

ELECTRIC PARKING BRAKE/HANDBRAKE

The phase one CIGs and BIGs were fitted with electric parking brakes when built. There was one unit fitted in each driving cab, plus an additional unit in the guard's compartment. The master switch had to be in the 'on' position to operate the mechanism. There were separate 'on' and 'off' switches and these were accompanied by a visual indicator which also displayed 'on' or 'off'. Each switch had to be held in for a few seconds before the mechanism was activated. The parking brake was situated under the motor coach and it could be heard winding on when activated from the guard's compartment. There were two backup systems which could be put into place if the parking brake failed to apply. The first involved winding a generator handle which was fitted to the mechanism in the guard's compartment. The BR1 key switch had to be turned 'on' for this process. The 'on' or 'off' switches could then be attempted whilst winding the handle in the correct direction, clockwise for 'on' and anticlockwise for 'off'. The second backup system was to hold the unit still by using the wheel scotches which were stored under the second man's seat in a locked red metal box. One box was to be found in each driving cab. The next step was to inform the fitters that the parking brake had failed.

The phase two CIGs, BIGs and all VEPs were built with the manual 'wheel' style of handbrake. There was one handbrake in each driving cab and each displayed a small red indicator when the handbrake was fully applied. There was also a manual locking device which held the handbrake wheel in place. A buzzer sounded in the cab if the driver attempted to take power with the handbrake applied.

Electric parking brake unit in the cab of phase one 4 CIG number 1711 (originally built as 4 BIG 7033). The 'on' and 'off' switches are positioned below the visual indicator which was a rotating disc that displayed 'on' or 'off' through a small glass window. The modern white box held the isolating switch for the train protection and warning system and the offside windscreen wiper valve can be seen to the left of this. *Ashley Barton*

27 PIN JUMPER AND SOCKET, BRAKE PIPE, MAIN RESERVOIR PIPE AND DUAL AIR COCKS

These items were stowed in receptacles on the front end of each unit. The 27 pin 70v jumper cable carried the control and auxiliary electrical connections between units. The jumper was situated beneath the second man's window while the socket was situated beneath the driver's window. The brake pipe and main reservoir pipe (which was fitted with star valves on the connectors) were both operated by red dual air cocks. The lowered position closed the cocks while the raised position opened them, allowing air to flow between units.

HEIGHT LIMITING BAR AND COLLECTOR SHOES

The height limiting bar was a wooden beam which was to be found on each side of the leading bogie. It was sometimes known as the 'shoe beam'. The shoe collected the current by sliding along the conductor rail. It was not actually attached to the height limiting bar. The bar stopped the shoe from moving too far upwards which would cause it to lose contact with the conductor rail. It also stopped it from dropping too low which could knock the shoe off when the train moved on to a new section of conductor rail. Occasionally, the height limiting bar could be knocked off or broken by an obstruction such as a fallen tree. In this instance, the shoe fuse would have to be removed and any remaining wreckage would be removed or tied up on to the bogie to keep it clear of the conductor rail.

SHOE/RIBBON FUSES

These copper fuses were fitted between the collector shoe and power train line and were located just behind the leading bogie at each end of a unit. If a shoe fuse had blown, the unit would need 'paddling up' i.e. inserting paddles (as described above) between the shoes and conductor rail. The driver could then change the fuse by loosening the securing bolts with a shoe fuse spanner. It was advised to tap the fuse with the back of your hand before removing it, just to make sure it was 'dead'! The muscles in your hand would contract if you grabbed the fuse while there was still a current running through it. This would not allow you to let go. A mistake like this could have been fatal!

A.W.S./T.P.W.S. RECEIVER, MAIN RESERVOIR TANK AND TOILET WATER TANK

These pieces of equipment were to be found mounted on the underframe. The main reservoir tank was easily recognised by its doughnut shaped valve.

A.W.S. AND D.S.D. ISOLATING COCKS

The A.W.S. and D.S.D. isolating cocks were positioned down near the buffer beam on the front near side of a unit.

The motor brake second equipment

This MBS was effectively the locomotive and as such it contained four traction motors and most of the mechanical and electrical equipment which was required to move the unit.

AUXILIARY CUPBOARD AND BRAKE VAN EQUIPMENT

The auxiliary cupboard was located in the guard's compartment. It was connected to the power train line via a power junction box. Spare fuses and shoe/ribbon fuses were carried in the right hand door of the cupboard which was divided into high and low tension sections.

The top section of the cupboard contained high tension fuses and the high tension auxiliary selector switch which was commonly known as the 'knife switch'. This switch had two positions, 'normal' and 'shed'. The 'normal' setting allowed the unit to take 750v dc from the conductor rail. The 'shed' setting allowed the unit to take 750v dc from an overhead shed supply via the shed sockets which were located at each end of the motor coach. The unit had to be 'cut out' (see page 56) when changing a high tension fuse. The high tension fuses were: line indicator (15 amp), compartment heat driving trailer x 2 (15 amp), van heat (15 amp), M.G. motor (60 amp), dummy heat (5 amp), compressor x 2 (30 amp), saloon heat driving trailer x 2 (15 amp), non-driving trailer heat (15 amp), and motor coach heat (15 amp).

The middle section of the cupboard contained a 70v fuse tester with a light bulb which illuminated if the fuse was in working order, the compressor governor switch, the compressor synchronisation switch and the control cut out switch (C.C.O.S.) which was used for isolating the traction motors. This section also contained nineteen miniature circuit breakers which were; emergency lights x 2, main lights x 5, control supply, loudaphone, starting bell, driving trailer auxiliaries, van light, lighting control, heating control, L.T. (M.G.) indicator (driving cabs), run back (camshaft back to the starting position), compressor control x 2, and personal address system.

The lowest section of the cupboard contained the compressor governor which would activate the compressors when the main reservoir air pressure dropped to 90lb/psi. The governor would cut out when the air pressure reached 100lb/psi. The system was protected by a safety valve which was set at 115lb/psi. When a train was formed with more than one unit, the compressor governors were synchronised through the compressor synchronisation wire. This was carried through the 27-pin control jumper. There was a member of staff whose job entirely consisted of moving around between depots to calibrate the compressor governors.

Some equipment was located on the outside of the auxiliary cupboard. This included a loudaphone, heating and lighting 'on' and 'off' switches, an ammeter which showed the amount of current being drawn from the conductor rail, the auxiliary isolating switch (A.I.S.) which, when set, allowed 750v dc to flow from the power train line or shed supply into the auxiliary cupboard. There was also a 'trip' switch to cut the supply. Using these switches was referred to as cutting the unit 'in' or 'out'. There was a B.R 1 key switch which energised the starting bell and personal address system. A rectangular blue button had to be depressed to activate the P.A. system. The guard could then make onboard passenger announcements using the telephone style handset which was also housed on the exterior of the cupboard. The switch also operated the electric parking brake on phase one units.

The guard's compartment also housed a brake valve, brake pipe gauge, brake cylinder gauge, track circuit operating clips, fire extinguisher and crowbar. There was a starting bell switch above each guard's compartment exterior door.

1963 stock auxiliary cupboard. Top half 750v; bottom half 70v. *Author's collection*

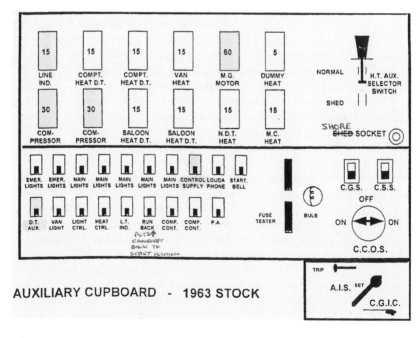

AUXILIARY CUPBOARD - 1963 STOCK

The brake van contained an emergency screw coupling, an escape ladder and an emergency cupboard which contained a first aid box plus a rope and saw which were used for tidying and tying up broken height limiting bars and collector shoes.

Most of the traction related equipment was carried on the underside of the motor coach. There were four 250hp axle hung, nose suspended traction motors (one per axle) which weighed in at over 1.5 tonnes each. The equipment carried on the underframe was as follows:

POWER TRAIN LINE

The power train line ran through the entire length of each four car unit. It carried the 750v dc supply from the collector shoes or shed supply, via power junction boxes (P.J.B.s), to the auxiliary cupboard and traction motors on the motor coach.

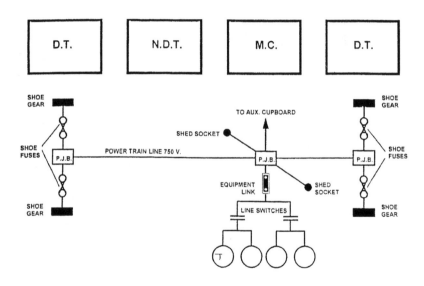

1963 stock power train line. The circles represent traction motors. *Author's collection*

EQUIPMENT LINK

The equipment link, also known as the 100 amp fuse, was in place between the auxiliary cupboard power junction box and the line switches. It was in place to protect the traction motors from excessive current.

LINE SWITCHES

The line switches were located between the equipment link and the traction motors. They were operated pneumatically by the 'control air' supply which had a separate reservoir and isolating cock on the underframe of the MBS. The switches would close when the driver moved the power handle away from the 'off' position. They would open to break the circuit when the driver placed the power handle back to the 'off' position. A 'pop' could be heard when they opened and a small ball of electricity would often be seen to drop down on to the track through the vents in the casing. The air operated movement of the switches was very quick so that minimal arcing was achieved as the contactors opened and closed. The 70lb/psi 'control air' supply also operated the camshaft, reversers and another set of electrical contactors.

REVERSERS

Each motor coach was fitted with two reversers, one for each motor bogie. The reversers altered the polarity to the traction motors depending on the direction of travel. They were operated by the reverser handle in the driving cab.

CAMSHAFT

The air/oil driven camshaft operated as each power notch was taken on the power handle. It rotated at a set speed and gradually increased the voltage to the motors. The traction motor overload device would operate if the voltage to the motors was applied too quickly. The camshaft quickly ran back to its starting position when the power handle was placed to 'off'.

RESISTANCES

The two banks of resistances were brought in and out of circuit depending on which power notch had been selected.

MOTOR GENERATOR (M.G.)

The motor generator ran as soon as the unit was 'cut in' with the auxiliary isolating switch. It converted the 750v dc line voltage down to the 70v required for the control circuit, main and emergency lighting circuits. It also charged the batteries.

BATTERIES

The batteries supplied limited power if the motor generator failed or stopped running due to line conditions. They supplied power to the control circuit, E.P. brake, headcode/tail lamp illumination and emergency lighting circuits. The batteries were recharged by the motor generator when the unit was in service.

COMPRESSORS

Each motor coach was fitted with two compressors which were driven by 750v motors when the master switch was in the 'on' position. They supplied compressed air to the main reservoir system from which air was taken for braking and various other applications which included the control air system, warning horn, windscreen wipers and toilet water raising system. The operation of the compressors was controlled by the compressor governor (see auxiliary cupboard).

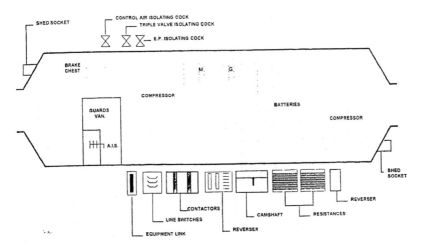

1963 stock motor coach traction equipment. *Author's collection*

Traction equipment on motor brake second 62033 from 4 CIG unit 1704 (originally built as 4 CIG unit 7317). The unit was photographed in Lover's Walk sidings on 30th January 2005, one of the two compressors being nearest to the camera. *Ashley Barton*

6

The braking systems

There were two types of braking system on 1963 units. The Westinghouse automatic air brake was operated from the brake pipe which in turn was charged by the main reservoir system. This brake was generally referred to as the autobrake. The electro-pneumatic (E.P.) brake operated with air taken directly from the main reservoir system. The two systems were interlinked via the driver's brake handle and each could be selected by operation of the brake selector switch which could be found in the driving cab (see chapter 4).

THE WESTINGHOUSE AUTOMATIC AIR BRAKE OR 'AUTOBRAKE'
The fail safe autobrake system operated the brakes, via a triple valve and auxiliary reservoir, when air pressure in the train brake pipe was lowered or was completely vented to 0lb/psi. The pipe was normally charged at 70lb/psi. This brake could only be lapped 'on'. If the driver required a lower brake application the brake had to be fully released and then reapplied once the brake pipe had recharged. This could take a few seconds and if misjudged, could have resulted in platform or signal overrun.

The driver could make a 'controlled' brake application by using the driving cab brake valve to lower the pressure in the brake pipe. The drop in air pressure began, near the brake valve, at the front of the train and gradually worked its way to the rear. The delay in application between the front and rear brakes applying along the length of the train often caused 'snatching' between vehicles and could be particularly noticeable on longer formations. The whole scenario would then be repeated when the brakes were released.

The triple valve controlled the flow of air between the auxiliary reservoir and the brake cylinders. In the 'release' position, the brake pipe air charged the auxiliary reservoir while the brake cylinder was connected to atmosphere (see fig. 1 below). The 'application' position (see fig. 2) closed the connection with the brake pipe and allowed air to flow from the auxiliary reservoir to the brake cylinders. The triple valve piston moved to the 'lap' position (see fig. 3) when the auxiliary reservoir pressure was reduced to equal the brake pipe pressure. This caused the air in the brake cylinders to become trapped thus holding the brakes on at the required level set by the position of the brake handle. When braking, a longer train required a larger volume of air to be exhausted from the brake pipe. An equalising discharge valve and reservoir catered for this and allowed the driver to make the same movements of the brake handle, regardless of the length of the train.

The brake pipe was linked into the driver's safety device, A.W.S./T.P.W.S. (see chapter 4), the guard's emergency brake valve and the passenger communication cord. If operated, all would trigger an 'uncontrolled' emergency brake application. The passenger communication cord was reset by turning a small red handle (butterfly) which was positioned at cantrail height on one end of each vehicle. The butterfly would turn by ninety degrees when the

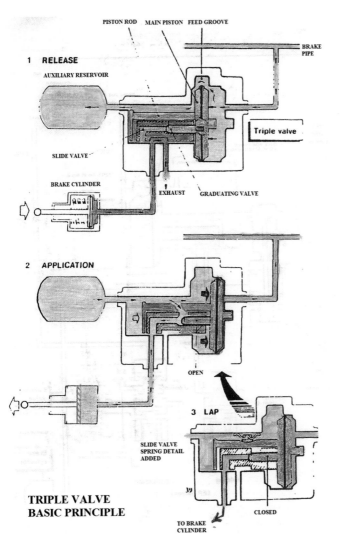

Cutaway diagram of the triple valve which was to be found in the brake chest on the underframe of each vehicle. *Author's collection*

cord was pulled, thus giving the train crew a visual indication as to which vehicle the cord had been pulled on. A rupture in the brake pipe would also trigger an emergency brake application.

THE ELECTRO-PNEUMATIC (E.P.) BRAKE

The E.P. brake operated directly from the main reservoir system via a series of valves, the most important of which were the application and holding valves. Air was applied to, or released from, the brake cylinders simultaneously along the length of the train. This eliminated snatching between vehicles and enabled the driver to make heavy, although smooth, brake applications which allowed for stopping over shorter distances. Unlike the autobrake, the E.P. brake could be lapped 'on' or 'off' to make adjustments in as many stages as the driver required. The main reservoir pressure was maintained by the compressors and these could often be heard running at a station when the driver had recently made a stop using the E.P. brake.

Basic diagram of the main air system on 1963 stock units. *Author's collection*

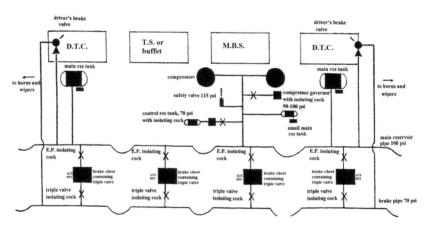

Driving techniques

This chapter describes the various techniques which were used by drivers when working in daily service on 1963 stock. Naturally, and probably due to their age, some units behaved in slightly differing manners. Most units were, however, very much attuned to each other. A rogue unit could be snatchy or pull away with a jerk. This could be more noticeable when running in multiple. The 'notching up' technique (see below) would usually compensate for this and rolling stock maintenance depots, on the whole, did an excellent job of keeping these units in good order. Failures in service were a rare occurrence. I was lucky enough to have a few runs on 4 CEP stock so I have included a short section on the five position brake handle as this differed somewhat from the three position handle to be found on 1963 stock.

POWER HANDLE NOTCHES
Notch 1 'Shunt'; the motors ran in 'series' with all resistances in circuit. *Series – All Motors were connected in a single path so that voltage was shared between them.*

Notch 2 'Series'; this gradually took out all resistances until full series was reached.

Notch 3 'Parallel'; all resistances were back in circuit and were gradually taken out until full parallel was reached. *Parallel – All motors were connected directly to the power source.*

Notch 4 'Weak field'; motors running in full parallel had the magnetic field around them weakened which allowed them to run at a higher speed. A slight snatch could be felt when a momentary drop and then surge of power occurred as weak field came in at 42mph. This snatching could be more prominent if the weak field was not quite synchronised between units that were running in multiple. If it was more comfortable to do so, the driver could place the power handle back to the notch one position once weak field had been attained. The power would remain 'on' until the handle was returned to the 'off' position.

ACCELERATING UNDER NORMAL DRIVING CONDITIONS
When pulling away under normal conditions it was usual to put the power handle to notch one and allow a little speed to build up. The driver would

then gradually work up through each notch until the desired speed was attained. The traction motor overload device would sometimes cut the power if it was applied too quickly.

It was best to place the power handle back to notch one before shutting the power off. Moving directly from a higher notch to 'off' would invariably cause the unit to jolt as the power dropped out.

Occasionally, a four-car unit would give quite a kick when pulling away. This would occur when working in the driving trailer furthest away from the motor coach. As power came in on the motor coach, the trailer second/buffet would be shoved forward into the driving trailer. The energy from the couplings squeezing up would then be released causing the front driving trailer to literally 'bounce' forward! The lurch would not be so noticeable, and may not happen at all, when driving the same unit from the driving trailer closest to the motor coach. Unfortunately, hand notching (see below) did not eliminate this problem as it would occur when taking notch one which applied the lowest possible amount of power to the motors. Leaving the brake on until the power came in, as for a start on an uphill gradient, sometimes worked to alleviate this problem. This kick did not occur when driving 3 COP units because the trailer vehicles were removed from the equation.

HAND NOTCHING; ACCELERATING UNDER POOR RAIL-HEAD CONDITIONS

A sticky sandy mixture called sandite was laid by specially equipped units in the autumn 'leaf fall' season. It was used in areas where noticeable adhesion problems affected acceleration and braking distances. Unfortunately, the solution only lasted for a short time before problems would recur. The hand notching technique allowed a driver to apply smaller than usual amounts of power to the traction motors when pulling away from a stand on contaminated rails. It helped to alleviate wheel spin, which if allowed to continue, would cause the traction motors to overload. When driving in these conditions it was good practice to open the cab window and listen for wheel spin as the power was applied. The technique could also be used if a unit was prone to overloading when accelerating.

When pulling away, the driver would place the power handle to notch one. The speed would then be allowed to build up gradually before placing the power handle to notch two and then quickly replacing it to notch one. The technique, which allowed the camshaft to apply power at a slower rate, could be employed approximately seven times before full series was achieved. The driver would allow a little speed to build up each time before repeating the movement. If required, the process could be run through again, this time by running the power handle backwards and forwards between notches one and three until full parallel had been achieved.

COASTING

Electricity is expensive, so for economical reasons, drivers were taught to 'coast' by placing the power handle to 'off' once the desired speed had been attained. Due to the weight and momentum of a train, fairly long distances could be covered before power was reapplied to the traction motors. Downhill gradients were utilised on many routes. For example; when leaving Falmer and heading towards Lewes, the driver would shut off the power at about 40mph as the train came out of Falmer tunnel. The gradient would do the rest and in a surprisingly short period of time the train would be running at the line speed of 70mph. At the opposite end of the scale, drivers would use uphill gradients to assist with braking, thus reducing wear and tear on the brake blocks.

Drivers were supposed to coast through conductor rail 'gaps' so as to avoid arcing. Gaps usually occurred in sidings or at junctions and crossovers where no collector shoes were in contact with the conductor rail. The location of conductor rail gaps was learned as part of a driver's route knowledge. A 'no volt relay' would cut the power to the traction motors if travelling over a gap with the power still applied.

WORKING OF THE WESTINGHOUSE AUTOMATIC BRAKE

The autobrake was mostly used when in training. When I first passed out as a driver, an instruction stated that it should be used when driving on empty stock workings, so as to keep in practice. Careful attention was needed at all times as this brake reacted more slowly than the E.P. brake. Its use was forbidden on passenger workings and eventually it was forbidden to use it unless the E.P. brake had failed. From then on, this brake was only used for running brake tests which were carried out when required by the rule book.

When stopping, an initial brake application was made to bring down the majority of the speed. The brake then had to be released to allow the brake pipe to recharge before a lower and gentler application was made to finish the stop. For a very smooth stop, the brake would be released and then reapplied at the moment of stopping. If an initial application was too light it could result in a hard stop. If too heavy, the driver would crawl up a platform at an embarrassingly slow rate before stopping the train gently. When in training, I can remember having to reapply power to reach the end of a platform on several occasions. The autobrake took quite a bit of mastering! You could tell if a driver was using the autobrake because a whoosh of air could be heard coming from the front of the train with each movement of the brake handle.

WORKING OF THE E.P. BRAKE

Under normal braking conditions the driver would initially apply approximately 15lb/psi to the E.P. brake. The application could then be increased or decreased as many times as was necessary. As with the autobrake, the E.P. brake would be released and then reapplied at the moment of stopping. The clicking of the application and holding valve relays was very prominent in the cab when a train was driven on the E.P. brake.

BRAKING UNDER POOR ADHESION CONDITIONS

Slippery railhead conditions could cause sliding and loss of adhesion when braking. As an indication to the driver, the speedometer would drop to '0' as the wheels locked. The brakes would then have to be released and reapplied, gently at first, so as to attempt to avoid a recurrence of the problem.

It was best to brake early in areas where poor adhesion was expected. Skill was required when driving these older units and a small initial brake application of approximately 5lb/psi would allow the brake blocks to clean any dirt from the wheel tyres. This could, and did, reduce the chances of sliding. Computers on modern disc braked units monitor each axle individually and control braking in such circumstances without intervention from the driver. The computer will release and re-apply the brakes on each affected axle in a pre programmed sequence. Noisy wheel flats were common in the autumn and the discerning traveller will notice that the computer controlled modern units, although programmed to prevent this problem, still suffer from this seemingly unavoidable and expensive nuisance.

FIVE POSITION BRAKE HANDLE AS FITTED ON CEP, BEP, EPB AND MLV

The 4 CEP units, later to become known as 'Kent Coasters' or 1957 stock, were built in stages for the Kent coast electrification scheme. Most of their working lives were spent on the South Eastern but they were also utilised on the Central and Western sections at various periods during their history. They were heavily refurbished during mid 1970s to mid 1980s and some were cut down to three car formations before eventual withdrawal. The units were capable of running at 90mph and were wholly compatible with 1963 stock.

They did have a heavier ride than '63s and the bogies were modified early on in an attempt to rectify this problem. The ride, at speed, did not always make them so popular with passengers. The heavier motor bogies were positioned, under the cabs, at each end of a unit. This made for an interesting ride for the driver although I personally found the whir of the motors rather comforting because their behaviour could be monitored at all times. This must have been very useful in the 'leaf fall' season. It wasn't always easy to hear if the wheels were spinning on the centrally located motor coach of a CIG, BIG or VEP unit.

The CEPs had another advantage over 1963 units. Should the need arise, a unit could still be driven with the motors isolated on one motor coach,

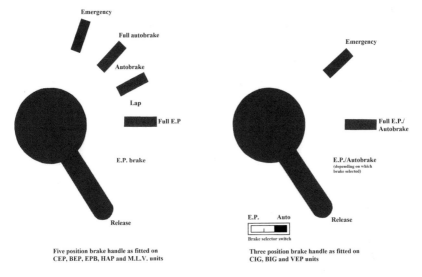

Emergency

Full autobrake

Autobrake

Lap

Full E.P

E.P. brake

Release

Five position brake handle as fitted on
CEP, BEP, EPB, HAP and M.L.V. units

Emergency

Full E.P./
Autobrake

E.P./Autobrake
(depending on which
brake selected)

Release

E.P.   Auto

Brake selector switch

Three position brake handle as fitted on
CIG, BIG and VEP units

Diagram of the five and three position brake handles. *Author*

The driving cab of a 4 CEP, unit number 7105. The five braking positions are clearly marked
out on the driver's desk. *Author*

provided the single motor generator was in working order. The motor bogies
could not be isolated separately on 1963 stock. The CEP power handles/
master switches worked in the same way as those fitted on phase two CIGs,
BIGs and all VEP units.

The five position brake handles were not as light to the touch as those fitted to 1963 units. They had a different feel and it took a little more time to get the hang of the various braking positions. There was no brake selector switch so the E.P. and auto brakes were selected by moving the handle to the corresponding positions marked out on the driver's desk. The positions beyond 'release' were as follows:

The E.P brake worked between 'release' and 'full E.P.' in exactly the same way as on the three position brake handle when the 'E.P.' brake had been selected.

The next position was 'lap' which was a sort of 'no man's land' between the E.P. and auto brakes.

The '0' to 'full service' autobrake came next. To apply it, the driver had to move the brake handle, very quickly, through 'E.P.' and 'lap' to the beginning of the autobrake position.

The 'emergency' brake was the last position and it worked, by dropping the brake pipe pressure to '0', in exactly the same fashion as that on the three position handle.

ATTACHING AND DETACHING UNITS

Making an attachment/detachment between units required a high level of concentration. The moves had to be carried out quickly if the train was in service on running lines. The buckeye couplings did not always engage on the first attempt and the emergency screw coupling had to be used if the units did not couple by the third attempt. With this in mind; it was usual practice to give the units a real bump on the second try. This would work ninety-nine times out of a hundred and use of the emergency coupling was a rare occurrence. The power handle was never placed to more than notch one 'shunt' and a unit was never moved until permission was given by the shunter.

To make an attachment, the driver would apply the power for a brief moment before gently coasting on to the other unit. Once the couplings had engaged, the driver would carry out a 'pull away' test by placing the unit in reverse and opening the power handle for a brief moment. The cab would then be shut down and the corridor connection opened. The main res. pipe, brake pipe and 27 pin jumper cable were connected between the units and the dual air cocks were opened. Some drivers used the loudaphone to inform the driver of the other unit that the attachment had been completed. Most drivers blew a long 'high' tone and long 'low' tone blast on the horn.

To make a detachment, the dual air cocks and corridor connections were closed and the pipes and jumper cable were disconnected. The cab of the unit to be detached was opened up and, on the shunter's instruction, the driver would pull forward to 'squeeze up' and release the tension on the couplings. The shunter would then open one coupling by pulling the release chain

4 VOP unit number 3901 (originally built as 4 VEP unit 7755) at Seaford on the 18th April 2005. The 27 pin jumper is on the left and the jumper receptacle is on the right. These are positioned in the recesses, alongside the brake and main reservoir pipes. The dual air cocks are in the lowered/closed position. *Author*

which was located under the buffer on the driving side of the unit. The driver would then set back and stop approximately six feet away from the other unit. The horn would then be blown twice, followed by a short pause, and then twice again, to inform the driver of the other unit that the detachment had been completed.

There were two ways of setting back when detaching units. The 'official' way was to momentarily apply the power in reverse before coasting backwards and stopping six feet away from the other unit. The 'unofficial' and usual way of doing it was much smoother. After the shunter had pulled the release chain, the brake was let off and the sprung Pullman style buffing plates would gently push the unit backwards before stopping.

Note: The driver who was not carrying out the attachment/detachment would take his E.P. key out of the master switch on his unit before the operation commenced. Multiple master switches turned 'on' would have caused serious problems with the braking system. There was a strict rule that only one E.P. key could be 'on' at any one time.

Practical handling, driver instruction and the driving exam

PRACTICAL HANDLING ON '63 STOCK

Having completed the training school courses, the Brighton trainmen were put on to a 'practical handling' course. This was at last a chance to do some driving, even if it was on empty stock which had been requisitioned for the training. Two men at a time went on the course and shared the driving. We completed two weeks on '63 stock and two days on 319 units. 319 training was necessary because the Brighton driving instructors all worked the Thameslink services to Bedford. Trainees with Brighton instructors spent a lot of time on Bedford runs so it took a lot longer for them to pass out. They still had to complete the required four hundred hours on '63 stock.

There was a suicide at Stoat's Nest Junction on our very first day of practical handling and we were delayed when travelling up to London to meet our instructor. Our train was diverted on to the slow line and we saw some unrecognisable body parts spread along the line. This was not the most auspicious start for our first day! Things went well after this and on each day we took it in turns to drive an 8-car train from London Victoria to Eastbourne and back. Although we had a fully qualified instructor, the train still had to have a competent driver on board. When not 'in the chair' we sat in a first class compartment chatting to the Victoria driver who was on a rather nice little number! We were trained to use the power handle carefully and at first spent a bit of time getting used to the E.P. brake. We were then introduced to the dreaded autobrake that we had heard so much about in the classroom. Our instructor, quite understandably, never really let 'us' take full control when driving on this brake. The course was really just a brief introduction to driving and most of our experience was gained with our driving instructors later on.

PRACTICAL HANDLING ON 319 UNITS

When learning how to drive 319s we managed two round trips per day between London Bridge and Tattenham Corner. Although simple to drive, the 319s were worked without a guard on the inner London services so we were required to operate the doors at stations. The units had comfortable driving cabs and a nice riding quality but as things turned out, I did not need to drive these units for quite some time (see chapter 11).

PLACEMENT WITH A DRIVING INSTRUCTOR

With basic training completed, I returned to Brighton and waited for placement with a driving instructor. The Brighton D.I.s had all been taken by the time I finished my practical handling and I was a little disappointed when I received a message telling me that I had been assigned to a Barnham D.I. This actually turned out to be a blessing in disguise for three reasons. Firstly, the driver that I was placed with was unbeatable as far as experience, knowledge and competence were concerned. Secondly, he had a great sense of humour and loved a practical joke which was always a good thing in what could sometimes be a very serious profession. Lastly, as explained above, the Brighton trainees spent a lot of time on 319s which meant that their required hours of driving on '63 stock took a lot longer. Four hundred hours of driving was required, with a minimum of one hundred worked on the autobrake. I had to calculate how many hours I had driven on each brake at the end of each day. I then filled out a record form which my D.I. would sign as proof of the time put in (see below).

Driving instructors were more commonly referred to as 'minders'. They were very competent train drivers who were paid a little extra to pass on their knowledge and skills. My minder had worked as a fireman in the days of steam and since then had driven electric trains for a long time. He had worked at Littlehampton depot for many years but this had been closed just prior to me being assigned to him. Littlehampton had been amalgamated with West Worthing and Bognor Regis to make a new 'super depot' at Barnham. The smaller depots were closed because the drivers were booking on remotely and could not be seen as 'fit for duty' by a train crew supervisor.

I was not allowed to book overtime when out with my minder and Barnham was an hour west of Brighton. With travelling time, I was generally lucky to get six hours driving completed in a day. This was still quicker than being with a 319 trained Brighton man. I would work out a suitable place to meet up with my minder and then let him know, in advance, where I would be. For instance, I would generally meet him at Hove if his first train was a Littlehampton to London Victoria service. I spent quite a lot of time travelling 'pass' to Barnham because a lot of his duties took us up the Mid-Sussex line or along the West Coastway to Portsmouth and Bournemouth.

THE FIRST DAY WITH MY MINDER

I first met my minder at Littlehampton, ten minutes before we had to work a morning commuter train up to London Bridge! We were working on Barnham duty number 7. A cushy little number which involved working from Littlehampton to London Bridge via Hove, then empty to Streatham Hill depot from where we would go 'pass' home. I was immediately put at ease by my minder's relaxed and congenial manner. He asked me to go and put his key on and get the 12 car train ready. He then disappeared for a few minutes to fetch his cup of tea and a newspaper. We talked a little as we got under way and I soon realised that he was reading the newspaper for most of the time, with just a glance out of the corner of his eye now and then to see that all was well. This put me at ease and I was given the odd instruction as to the location of braking marks or the commencement of a speed restriction. This was the first time that I 'officially' drove a train with passengers on board.

We gradually made our way along the West Coastway towards Hove. From there, we took the Cliftonville Spur which avoided Brighton and took us on to the main line to London at Preston Park. I did not use the autobrake other than when performing running brake tests. The trip went very well and once away from the coast there were longer runs between stations so I managed to get a bit of speed up. We arrived at London Bridge more or less on time which was actually not a bad feat on any day during the rush hour! We then changed ends to take the units empty to Streatham Hill sidings. I set up the cab and got the driver's seat into a comfortable position. The signalman phoned and informed me that the Sydenham Spur was blocked by a class 455 unit. The spur came off the main line and ran around to Crystal Palace and then on to Streatham Hill. The unit was stuck, due to the greasy railhead conditions, on the gradient that led up to the short viaduct which crossed over the main line. The autumn leaf fall season had recently begun. The signalman asked me if I knew my way via 'the hills'. I did not know what 'the hills' were, and with a look of alarm, I promptly shoved the phone into my minder's hand! He informed the signalman that he did indeed know the way and a moment later we got the signal to leave. We left London Bridge and crossed over on to the slow lines from where we headed on to the South London Line at South Bermondsey Junction. We then headed towards Peckham Rye where my minder said that the route indicator on the junction signal was 'hopefully' pointing the right way to Tulse Hill. He asked me to keep the speed right down and after running through East and North Dulwich stations we did actually arrive at Tulse Hill, where we pottered through the platform towards another junction indicator. My minder then announced that he 'thought' the indicator on the signal was showing the correct route. I looked at him with my eyebrows raised and he smiled and said "Should be alright, though last time I did all this I was firing on a steam engine!" Bearing in mind that you had to re-learn and re-sign for a route after six months of not driving on it, this was quite a feat of memory and was also quite against the rule book! I looked at him and smiled. I could see that we were going to get on well! Luckily, the right route 'had' been set and after

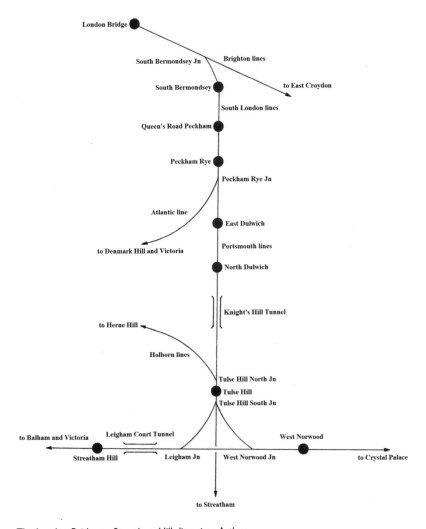

The London Bridge to Streatham Hill diversion. *Author*

berthing the train in the shed at Streatham Hill, we made our way to Clapham Junction where we boarded the first train heading south. With my first day's driving behind me, and the knowledge that I was in good hands, I parted company with my minder at Hove and made my way home. Things quickly settled into a routine and we became good friends. What follows is a list of the routes covered at the time by the 'top link' men at Barnham. My minder was in this link so it is also a list of the routes that I covered when learning to drive:

Brighton to Portsmouth Harbour including Littlehampton and Bognor Regis (West Coastway)

Brighton to London Victoria/London Bridge

Farlington Junction to Bournemouth via Southampton, including the diversionary route via Botley and Eastleigh

Ford to Three Bridges via Horsham (Mid-Sussex Line)

Norwood Junction and Sydenham Spurs to Balham via Crystal Palace and Streatham Hill

THE MID-SUSSEX LINE

The Mid-Sussex line is a very scenic route but it was also probably the hardest to drive along, due to the amount of downhill gradients on the approaches to stations. This made it particularly difficult during the leaf fall season and early braking was very much the norm in the autumn. Pulling away from stations could also be tricky. You had to have the cab window open, to listen out for wheel spin, no matter what the weather. If this was the case, the power would have to be shut off before making another attempt to get away. It could take quite some time to get moving and build up the required amount of speed. There are also a lot of curves; in fact there are very few straight lengths of track at all. Combining this, with mostly semaphore signalling, you very much had to have your wits about you, especially in the dark. Unlike the Brighton line, which is mostly well illuminated, the Mid-Sussex runs through a dark and rural area. Braking marks were a lot harder to find in the pitch black of a moonless night. It was imperative that you kept a very sharp eye out for the semaphore home signals which foretold the approach of a station.

BRIGHTON, LITTLEHAMPTON AND VICTORIA

I didn't get to drive on many of the Brighton to Portsmouth Harbour stoppers because these were mostly covered by the lower link Brighton and Barnham drivers. They were, however, good for braking practice because there were about thirty stations along the route. We did sometimes get to Portsmouth if working down the Mid-Sussex line from Victoria but these services tended to run semi-fast along the coast. A lot of time was spent on Littlehampton and Brighton to London Victoria workings, with the occasional fast Brighton to Victoria thrown in for good measure. These fast services were great fun to drive and for a while were branded with the grand title of the 'Capital Coast Express.' Dedicated trains were formed of semi-permanently coupled 4 CIG and 4 BIG units. These were reclassified as 8 DIG which stood for 'Dedicated Intermediate Guard'. They carried a small 'CCE' logo on the cab side with a larger one on the brake van (see below).

8 DIG 2002, formed from units 1902 and 2254 (originally built as 7325 and 7382/7036 respectively), departs platform six at Brighton with an up 'Capital Coast Express' working to London Victoria in April 1996. *Tony Yardley*

With a schedule of about fifty minutes for the journey, and with only one stop at East Croydon, it was great to open up the power handle and 'Give it the gun!' which my minder would say as we pulled away!

BOURNEMOUTH, PIGEONS, TUNNELS, M.C.B.S AND PADDLES

The top link at Barnham had the lion's share of Bournemouth work, although the first train down in the morning and last train back at night were both worked by top link Brighton men. The Bournemouth turns soon became a favourite, and with regular runs, I learned the road well enough for my minder to sit back and let me get on with it. We would chat a lot, and with his particular liking of wildlife, I soon learned to pick out various kinds of deer and birds as we hurried through the New Forest. My minder loved musicals and would occasionally tap dance and sing while running at speed. A surreal experience!

I remember a funny incident that happened when driving back on a return trip from 'Bomo' as it was known. I was running at speed on green signals between Fareham and Portchester whilst my minder was dozing comfortably in the sun. He jumped out of his skin as we hit two wood pigeons with a split second between them! The bangs on the reinforced fibreglass front of the unit were exceptionally loud. I had seen that the inevitable was going to happen but did not have time to give any warning! Hitting pigeons was a regular occurrence and it was something that you unfortunately had to get used to, along with the rest of the wildlife that happened to stray on to the line. I later struck a pigeon at 90mph between Clayton and Patcham tunnels. The poor bird had its head jammed between the two struts which made up the windscreen wiper arm. Death must have been instantaneous but the pigeon would not dislodge. It flapped around on the front of the unit for the rest of the journey to Brighton where I removed it from the wiper arm, minus most of its feathers!

I quickly found out that being made to jump was a thing that I would have to get used to! Being a great practical joker, and when I was least expecting it, my minder would wait until we went in to a tunnel and hit the wall of the cab, right next to my head, with a wooden paddle! The first time that this happened was in Clayton tunnel and I let go of the deadman's handle which applied the emergency brake. The speed dropped by about 40mph by the time I had shut off power, re-set the handle, and waited for the brakes to come off! For a change, he would sometimes lean over and stroke my earlobe or put his face right next to my head which made me jump as we came back into the light! He would also switch out the 'main control' M.C.B. behind my head, usually while I was looking out of the window, waiting for the guard to ring the bell at a station. I would then open up the power handle and we would begin to roll backwards because the M.C.B. had cut the control circuit out! He always picked an uphill gradient for this stunt. I soon learned to flick the switch back in without even looking at it! Sometimes he would knock my hand off the power handle if I was looking out of the side window. We came to a grinding halt on one occasion because the train wasn't moving very quickly. I can only imagine what the guard and passengers must have thought of this! This light-hearted mischief taught me to stay calm and not be nervous in the cab. Unexplained thumps and bumps occasionally occurred, especially when driving at speed. It also taught me to recover from unexpected emergency brake applications which did happen now and then. It was all a good grounding for when I was to go out driving on my own and I always remembered what my minder told me to do, should something untoward happen in the future. "You should always take one minute to roll a cigarette, relax, and think through what you are going to say or do before talking to anybody." It was good advice and it taught me to keep a cool head in all situations. Incompetent signalmen however, did sometimes cause some frustration. I was taught how to insult signalmen who had held us up for no apparent reason. When approaching the offending signal box you would blow 'Derrr-Durgh!' on the horn which, when roughly translated into English, meant 'Arrrr-soles!' Another neat little trick that he taught me was to place the pastie that I had taken in for dinner on the heater in the rear cab so that it could slow cook on the outward journey! No thermostats were fitted to the cab heaters on '63 stock so they were either 'on' or 'off.' Situated directly

4 CIG 1706 (originally built as unit 7319) stands in platform one at Bournemouth, 14th July 1994. The 46 headcode was used on Victoria – Bournemouth services which ran via Hove. *Ashley Barton*

below the driver's seat, your rear end would cook while your legs and feet froze, especially if there was a draught under the dashboard!

Bournemouth trips were extremely good for a driver in training. There were plenty of sections where you could get up a bit of speed, balanced with just enough stations to keep your hand in on the autobrake. The approach to Swanwick is on a downhill gradient and on one occasion my first application was way too late. I hit the platform ramp at 50mph with the brake in 'full service'. The '63 stock generally had very good brakes and, true to form, the unit stopped right on the 4 car mark as I let the brake off for a gentle stop. Things like this would happen occasionally and your toes would uncontrollably curl up in your shoes! I sometimes had a bad day on the autobrake in the early days. Nothing happened that was dangerous, it was just poor technique or bad timing which would result in heavier braking than I would have liked. My minder would reassuringly say that it would come in time. This it did, but it took a couple of months to really get the hang of it.

The service would sometimes be terminated at Southampton if we were running late. This would involve a platform to platform shunt before setting out on the return journey. If carrying on to Bournemouth, we would pass the Freightliner terminal near Redbridge and then run through Totton before opening up the power and heading through the forest to Brockenhurst. After leaving Brockenhurst, the line runs through New Milton where we were occasionally booked to stop. If not stopping it was possible to get some real speed up because the line is on a falling gradient to Christchurch. This stretch was where I clocked my fastest ever speed with a 4 CIG unit. I hurtled through Hinton Admiral at 96mph! My minder commented something along the line of "Blimey, we're shifting a bit!" but I just shrugged and replied "Just on the line speed!" He wasn't silly and knew that I was over the top of the actual 90mph speed restriction! Just for the record, I would like to add that I was normally very conscientious where speed was concerned. This kind of thing didn't happen very often and we must have had full-sized wheels and the wind behind us to achieve that kind of speed. It would certainly not be sensible with modern units because all are fitted with a black box recorder. Providing that the speed restrictions allowed for it, 90mph on '63s was always achievable when driving in 'weak field' on the right stretch of track. Moving on to an uphill gradient would quickly demonstrate that there was very little power to spare with the motors running 'flat out' in weak field.

CLASS 33 FIRE

An unusual incident happened whilst heading up the Brighton line on a hot summer's day. On approach to Redhill, we noticed a freight train disappearing into the distance ahead of us. The platform signal took some time to clear and while waiting we discussed what possible reason the signalman could have had to put a slow freight in front of a class one train. We decided that it was probably a signalling error and it certainly was as far as we were concerned!

We left Redhill running on yellow cautionary signals. Our speed increased gradually but the freight train cannot have been moving at more than about 45mph. We were still running on yellows when we noticed a very small fire on the ballast as we ran into Merstham Tunnel. On a normal day you could see out of the far portal but today the tunnel was dark and fume ridden. We assumed that the loco was working very hard indeed. As we progressed, we noticed more and more little fires which were now burning between the running rails. As we exited the tunnel I contacted the signalman with the cab radio. I explained the situation and he informed me that he would pass the message on to 'Control'. He also said that we would get past the freight at Stoat's Nest Junction because it was booked to stay on the slow line and we were booked to cross over on to the fast. We passed many more fires and were finally stopped at the signal which protected the junction. Ahead of us, the freight had come to a stand with the tail end fouling the junction's track circuit. The reason for the fires was now obvious. Clouds of thick, black, oily smoke were pouring out from beneath the class 33 locomotive at the front of the train. This was accompanied by the occasional lick of flame which was jetting out sideways! I called the signalman again but he already knew about the fire. He told me that the fire brigade were due to arrive at any minute and that the current was about to be switched off. The line indicator in the cab went to 'off' so my minder applied the handbrake and informed the guard that we were going to be delayed for some time. We would probably have got away with it if the freight had just cleared the track circuit by a few yards. The fire brigade arrived quickly and they duly buried the underside of the loco in foam. It must have been very hot because smoke continued to pour out for quite some time. The weather was also hot and the passengers on our train became restless. A few people threatened to get down on to the track and make their own way when they saw us escort a member of the public from the train to a waiting taxi. The man was a surgeon who was on his way to perform an important operation at St Thomas's Hospital in London. We explained this to the passengers who were, on the whole, very patient. In the end, we sat there for just over two hours until the current had been restored and the freight moved away from the junction.

I discovered what had happened on the following day. The loco had been pulling a heavy load of ballast spoil. The traction motors had got hot enough to ignite a large build up of old grease and oil which had accumulated on the underside. The poor Redhill driver, whose misfortune it had been to be working the train, had only just passed out on 33s and it was the first time that he had been out with one on his own! He must have cursed his luck, for 33s normally had a reputation of being very reliable locos.

THE DRIVING TEST

My minder was assigned to another trainee when I had completed a little more than the required four hundred hours in the cab. We parted company as good friends and I returned to Brighton to apply for my driving test. I had to wait for a couple of weeks until an examiner was available and on the day before my test I went out for a quick refresher with another Barnham minder. I met him at Worthing from where I drove up to Victoria and back down to Hove. One of my mates had passed his driving test on this day and he had really had a time of it. He had made his way to Victoria to meet his examiner and had then driven from Victoria to East Grinstead and back, twice with an eight car train! Almost the entire test had been completed using the autobrake. He had been asked a lot of traction and rules questions whilst driving so it really must have been hard to concentrate on the braking. He returned to Brighton mentally exhausted. I went home glad in the knowledge that I had a different examiner booked for my test! I had spent a total of 146 hours and fifty-five minutes on the autobrake, with a grand total of 430 hours and fifty-one minutes driving on 1963 stock.

The day of my driving test arrived. To my surprise, my examiner was ready and waiting at Brighton when I booked on for duty. More surprisingly, he asked me where I would like to drive a train to! I asked him if it would be OK to drive to Littlehampton and he nodded and went to look for the driver

DIs NAME P. HALL — SATUR/MON DAY/DATE 29·06·96 / 01·07·96

TIME ON	TIME OFF	STOCK	Total hours WC	Total hours EP	Total hours Auto	HOURS DRIVING DAY	HOURS DRIVING DARKNESS	DOO	
1648	2248	1963		1HR	2HRS	3HRS			BH 205 B
AP 0830	1630	1963		2HRS	1HR40	3HRS40			BH 29

TOTAL 430 HRS 51 MINS.

DIs NAME P. HALL — WEDS/THURS DAY/DATE 03/05·07·96

TIME ON	TIME OFF	STOCK	Total hours WC	Total hours EP	Total hours Auto	HOURS DRIVING DAY	HOURS DRIVING DARKNESS	DOO	
0830	1630	1963		C	T	C	THEN SPARE		BH 29
0558	1358	1963		2HRS	1HRSm	3HRS Sm			BH8

DIs NAME P. HALL — FRI/SATUR DAY/DATE 06·07·96

TIME ON	TIME OFF	STOCK	Total hours WC	Total hours EP	Total hours Auto	HOURS DRIVING DAY	HOURS DRIVING DARKNESS	DOO	
0800	1600	1963		2HRS	2 amins	2HRS20			BH 2009

DIs NAME P. HALL — TUESDAY/DATE 09·07·96

TIME ON	TIME OFF	STOCK	Total hours WC	Total hours EP	Total hours Auto	HOURS DRIVING DAY	HOURS DRIVING DARKNESS	DOO	
0558	1358	1963		2HRS	2HRS	4HRS		✓	BH 17

DIs NAME — DAY/DATE

TIME ON	TIME OFF	STOCK	Total hours WC	Total hours EP	Total hours Auto	HOURS DRIVING DAY	HOURS DRIVING DARKNESS	DOO	
PART 3	EXAM	– EXAMINER	IAN	SIMMONS					
PASSED	1st TIME	–	I'VE	GOT	MY	KEY.			

SPECIFIC BRAKE HANDLING RECORD

PRACTICAL TRAIN HANDLING AUTOMATIC BRAKE 100 HOURS				
DATE	DIAGRAM NO.	TIME	TOTAL TO DATE	DIs SIGNATURE
03·07·96	BH 27	C T C		
05·07·96	BH8	1 HRS	144·35	P Hall
06·07·96	BH 2009	20 MINS	144·55	P Hall
09·07·96	BH 17	2 HRS	146·55	P. Hall

The last two pages of my specific brake handling record. 'AP' on the second line of the top form stands for 'Attach Portion'. A record of attachments/detachments had to be kept. 'CTC' stands for 'Croydon Training Centre'. Trainees occasionally had to go to Croydon for one-day courses. *Author's collection* who was booked to work the next service. The route was a hastily made choice but I knew the West Coastway very well so it seemed a wise one. It was a 45-minute run on a stopping service to Littlehampton. There were plenty of stops and with a four car train I was hoping that my test was going to be easier than my mate had had on the previous day. The driver of the train that we commandeered went 'pass' back to Barnham because it was his last working of the day. He had started early so we had done him a small favour.

My examiner took me down to platform three where a 4 CIG unit was waiting on the stops. I opened up the cab, carried out a personal brake test and then called the guard, via the loudaphone, for a train brake test. This completed, I wound the roller blinds to display the correct headcode (64) and settled into the seat to wait for the signal and starting bell. My examiner, a fairly young and friendly fellow, politely asked me if I was going to set up the cab secure radio. My heart sank; I had made a mistake already! He smiled and said, "Try to relax; you've done this hundreds of times before so just treat today as if it was a normal working day". It was good advice and I decided to treat the situation as if my minder was sitting in the second man's seat rather than an examiner. The guard rang 'two' on the bell and I pulled out of the platform and ran through the crossovers which led on to the down line. I carried out a running brake test and blew the horn as I entered Hove tunnel. The first stop, at Hove, was carried out using the E.P. brake so that I could get the feel of the unit. At this point, my examiner said "I would like to see you make four or five stops on the autobrake. Just choose which stations you like before we get to Littlehampton". The first stop that I selected was Southwick. The platform was longish and so it didn't matter too much if I was a few feet from the four car stop mark. I braked, a little too lightly at first, and made a bit of a hard stop. This made the examiner laugh. It was right on the mark though! I managed about half a dozen more stops on the autobrake. I had begun to relax and so the braking improved and the stops were gentler. I shut the cab down and applied the handbrake when we arrived at Littlehampton. I thought it would be best to stay on the safe side because I was under observation. It usually took a few hours for the brake air to leak off on '63 stock. Applying the handbrake unnecessarily could upset the next driver who was booked to work the unit, especially if he was cutting it fine after a tea break! My examiner kindly complemented me on my driving and informed me that we were going to run through preparation and disposal on a unit which was berthed in the sidings.

We made our way over to the wash road, where another 4 CIG was waiting on the stops. We walked around the outside of the unit and I was asked to point out the underside equipment before climbing up into a cab. The unit was 'flat' (no air in the system) so I demonstrated how to pump it up by putting the E.P. key on to charge the brakes. I then walked through the unit and carried out train preparation duties (see appendix 1). I pointed out the various bits of equipment by name as we passed them. This completed, I carried out disposal which consisted of shutting the cab down, applying the handbrake and checking that the correct roller blinds were displayed before turning the lights out. I asked my examiner if he knew how effective the handbrakes actually were. To demonstrate, he put his key on and put the power handle to notch 4, weak field. The 1000hp CIG was like an enormous dog straining at its lead, having seen a rabbit disappear down a hole. It was quite an incredible tug of war and I felt sure that the CIG would lurch forward into the buffers! To the handbrake's credit, the unit did not move one inch. With this demonstration over, the examiner smiled and handed me an E.P. key. He said I could keep it 'if' I could keep him in one piece on the short run to Worthing, where he happened to live! We commandeered the next stopping train to Worthing and I drove mostly on the E.P. brake, so as to keep my key! We then handed the train back to its driver and I shook hands with my examiner as he congratulated me on passing my test and wished me luck for the future. I stayed on the train to Brighton and informed the T.C.S. that I had passed out for driving. I could now enter the relief driver's link and begin a job that I had waited a very long time for. I went home by train, twirling my newly earned E.P. key in my hand. I was elated at having passed without the stress that my mate had been put through on the preceding day. I called my minder to thank him and let him know the good news. He had shared a huge amount of knowledge, always with kindness, patience and occasional unflinching bravery! Through the years, although still based at Brighton, I was to become a driver for Network SouthCentral, Connex South Central and Southern Trains.

THE MASTER OR 'E.P.' KEY

The master key was known as an 'E.P.' key on the Southern Region, the E.P. standing for 'electro-pneumatic'. Being the equivalent of a pilots 'wings', the E.P. key was only allowed to be carried by a driver after passing his or her driving test. A trainee was not allowed to be in possession of one. The key was very important but it had a very simple function. It was used to unlock the master switch which could then be moved to the 'on' position. The key could only be removed once the master switch was placed in the 'off' position. If a driver was relieved during a journey, he would be passed the relieving driver's key to save shutting the train's circuits down unnecessarily. Drivers would probably exchange keys at least once on a shift. This meant that a driver would probably use thousands of keys during his or her career. A driver was only supposed to be in possession of one key. In reality, it was sensible to obtain another, just in case of accidental loss or emergencies. I was once shown an illegally doctored key by one of my supervisors. He was doing a spot check to make sure that nobody was in possession of one.

The key had been filed or cut down so that it could be removed from the master switch once it had been placed to 'on'. A single driver, who possessed one of these keys, could get many units ready for service at the same time. This, of course, would mean that the units would have to be left unattended in a 'ready to drive' state. A driver was never allowed to leave a train unattended if it was ready for service. Naturally, rules were made to be broken and an occasional quick visit to the toilet would be required before setting off. The cab doors would always be locked, so as to be on the safe side! I never saw a doctored key in use and I am certain that they were a throw-back from the earlier days of multiple locomotive working where the compressors on both locos could be pumped up simultaneously to save time.

An area manager presented me with a certificate and another E.P. key some months after passing out as a driver. It came complete with a 'Network SouthCentral Training Centre' key ring which was embossed on the rear face with the inscription: 'DRIVER T.WOOD BRIGHTON'

Presentation E.P. key and key ring. *Author*

9

Routes and Links

ROUTE LEARNING AS A RELIEF DRIVER

Drivers in the relief/starter link only got paid the driver's rate of pay if they actually did some driving. It was best to get a few of the shorter routes out of the way first. You would then have a chance to get some driving behind you, with the added bonus of having a driver's wage thrown in. Brighton to Seaford was the first route that I learned. My traction inspector gave me photocopied plans of the route and informed me that I had one week in which to complete the task. The plans, although accurate as far as the track layouts were concerned, were fairly basic so I added the details as I went along (see below). Speed restrictions, braking points, signalling moves, shunt moves, signal box area codes, level crossings and the location of line side phones were all added to the maps. Adding 'in-depth' detail helped the route to sink in, although it would soon become obvious that I only really learned a route by driving over it myself. This being the case, it was always good to get a driver who would let me take the controls for a bit. This was against the rules but it was good to get as much experience as possible before driving over a new route on my own. I also had to learn local instructions which were contained in the 'Sectional Appendix.' This book contained very basic track plans of running lines, speed restrictions and junctions. Adding the exact locations of speed restrictions to the photocopies was a more accurate way of learning. The local instructions at the back of the book were much more informative and they included details of where permissive working was permitted (more than one train allowed in a section at one time). The Seaford branch had its own local instruction which stated that a driver should not apply more than notch two 'series' when driving more than one four-car unit. This was due to the remoteness of the substation at Newhaven.

I went for a couple of runs in the dark so that I could learn which lights were signals and which were domestic lighting. The home signal at Newhaven Harbour was the only one that was hard to distinguish. Strangely enough, this was the signal that I had found hard to pull off years before when doing work experience. The dull lamp of the semaphore signal was right in front of the Newhaven-Dieppe ferries' landing stage. The ferry had red and green port and starboard lights so care had to be taken! I completed the task and my traction inspector questioned me about the route before signing me off as 'competent' to drive over it.

I was called upon to work a Seaford train within a couple of days of signing the route. Unfortunately, the head traction inspector noticed the T.C.S. giving me the train schedule. He decided that he was coming along for the ride as it was my first time out and he had nothing better to do! We chatted as I drove the train but I didn't really feel that I had done it on my own. On arrival back at Brighton I asked the T.C.S. if I could work a 'fiddle' and take another train over to Seaford. He agreed and another driver got to go home early.

I was soon walking up the platform to do my first solo run with a 4 CIG unit. This time I was a little nervous, even more so than doing it with the head traction inspector in the cab! Once ready, the guard rang 'two' on the bell and I gently pulled away from platform 8. The first time that I looked to the right hand side of the cab for my minder was as I rolled through the points of Montpelier Junction, just outside the station! It was very strange to sit alone in the cab with all of the responsibility to myself. There was nobody to turn to for advice when I was unsure about something. Looking to my right, and remembering that there was nobody there, happened occasionally during the next few months. It eventually stopped as my confidence built up. Fired on adrenalin, the run to Seaford went well. The return trip also went well until I forgot the braking mark for Falmer. On approach to the station, the brakes would normally be applied about half way along the

4 CIG 1732 (originally built as 7321) stands in the Wall siding at Lewes after being taken out of service due to a brake fault, 15th March 1994. The siding was occasionally used during severe service disruption or for stabling defective rolling stock. Memorising shunt moves, into and out of sidings, was an important part of the route learning process. *Ashley Barton*

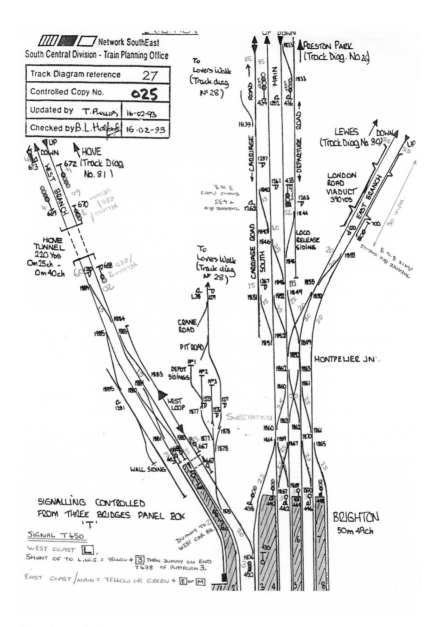

Route diagram for Brighton. The photocopied route learning sheets had to be detailed with speed restrictions, signalling routes and shunt moves etc. Adding these details helped with learning the route. *Author's collection*

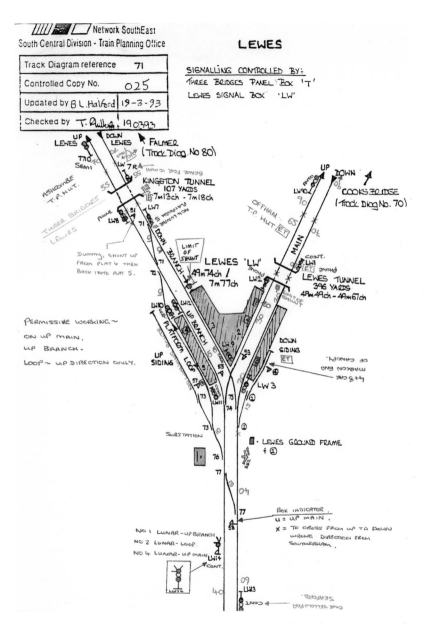

Route diagram for Lewes. The signal box is coloured in orange and speed restrictions are red. *Author's collection*

length of the tunnel. I did not apply them until I came out of the far portal and saw the platform ramp ahead! I threw the brake handle into 'full service' and luckily the train stopped, rather abruptly, on the 4 car mark. The lesson was learned and I never again forgot where the braking mark was! I was a little shaken for a moment but I had to carry on and put the mistake down to experience. It was a good feeling to roll up to the stops at Brighton with my first run behind me. I went home with mixed feelings that evening. On the one hand, I was pleased with myself for finally driving a train on my own. On the other, I was cross with myself for making a daft mistake which nearly caused me to over-run a station.

LOVER'S WALK DEPOT AND SIDINGS

I took advice from the other drivers and next learned Lover's Walk depot. This was a requirement early on because shunt moves within the depot, and between the station and depot, went on around the clock. Guards were not required in the sidings and back in those days a driver was paid £10 D.O.O. (driver only operation) money as soon as a train was moved without a guard on board. It could be a lucrative week with just one shunt move per day! The down side was that some T.C.S.s would save on costs by only giving the senior relief drivers some driving work. Others were great and would try to get us all some work if they could.

Only one day was allowed for learning Lover's Walk depot. In reality, that was what it took to learn the mere basics. 'Depot protection' was explained on site by my traction inspector. This was put in place to protect workers within the carriage shed. A flashing light at the buffer stops end of a shed road would warn that no movements were permissible because staff could be working on the units occupying that particular road. There was a locked case near the buffers and a train could only be moved once all of the workers had removed their tags from it and the light extinguished.

Most of the shed roads were fed by an overhead power supply. This was fed to a train via a jumper cable which plugged into the exterior 'shed supply socket' on a motor coach. A driver would require the shunt signal to be 'off' for his road when moving out of the shed. This signal could only be cleared once the derailer outside the shed was disabled. The shunter's permission was then needed to pull out of the shed and on to the conductor rail where the driver would halt the train at a stop board. The shed supply jumper cable would then be removed before the shunter could give permission for the driver to continue with the movement. A train formed with more than one unit could be a little sluggish when pulling out of the shed because there was a slight uphill gradient. The power would increase as each unit came on to the conductor rail. Care had to be taken when applying the power so as to avoid severe arcing from the rear units as their collector shoes approached the conductor rail.

4 CIG 1724 (originally built as 4 BIG 7039) stands outside '10 shed' at Lover's Walk depot in the summer of 2003. *Ashley Barton*

A train would be stopped on a shunt signal before entering the shed. Once clearance was given, the shunter would push a button which would disable the derailer and clear the signal. The shunter would then instruct the driver to pull up to the shed entrance, stop, blow the horn, and then proceed. The overhead supply was not used because trains were rolled into the shed on the downhill gradient. The batteries would supply power to the E.P. brake once a unit came away from the conductor rail. Care had to be taken when running in and speed had to be kept down to 5mph. A handbrake was always applied to a unit before leaving it. If on an electric parking brake unit, most drivers would flick the 'on' switch well before the buffers as these brakes took some time to apply. All movements within the shed would trigger the siren and overhead warning lights for the road in use. There were also warning lights in the pits on the inspection roads.

Once depot protection had been explained it was down to me to walk around with a track plan and learn where shunting signals were positioned. It helped to ride in and out on units and it was even better if you were allowed to drive a few. It took quite some time to learn the myriad of shunt moves within the depot and out to the station. Even after a few years of experience you could still come across a move that you were not aware existed.

There were three carriage roads for movements between the station and depot: the main carriage road, the South carriage road and the West carriage

4 VEP 3514 (originally built at 7837) stands on number one Lover's Walk sidings. This siding was commonly known by drivers and depot staff as 'One Lover's'. In the background can be seen the twelve road carriage shed and the depot's resident class 09 is coupled to a 1963 stock DTC on number one shed road. 26th July 2002. *Chris Wilson*

road which only allowed movements between the depot and platform two. The blanket speed restriction of 5mph had only two exceptions. If the main line was not in use, passenger trains could be driven at 15mph on the main carriage road between Preston Park and Brighton. The carriage washer had a maximum speed of 3mph. A higher speed would damage the flails but there was a snag with this. Because of the uphill gradient, a four car unit moving at less than 5mph would not make it to the conductor rail on the far side of the washer! I managed to 'gap' a unit thus while being allowed to drive another driver's train. It was embarrassing to say the least and we needed the depot signal cabin's permission to roll back and have another go! Drivers were constantly reminded by traction inspectors that the 3mph speed limit should be adhered to. All of them were ex-drivers and knew that it was not actually possible! A convenient blind eye was turned or the job would have come to a standstill. There were quite a few conductor rail gaps within the depot and learning their location was very important. Most were four car gaps but there was also an eight car one. A unit stranded thus would normally be pushed back onto the 'juice' by another unit. If a collector shoe was very close but not actually in contact with the conductor rail, a less than safe method was sometimes employed. The gap would be bridged by placing a short circuiting bar between the collector shoe and conductor rail!

Lover's Walk also had two sets of open-air sidings. Sidings one to three 'Lover's Walk' were just north of the carriage shed and one to six 'Montpelier' were between the shed/workshops and the main line. It was very important to learn how many cars fitted in each siding. The signaller in the depot signal cabin had to keep a constant record of how many cars were berthed in each siding. Taking an eight car train into a twelve car road which was already occupied by another eight would be embarrassing and could also have caused delays. There were also shunt necks to the north of the signalling cabin and these were sometimes used for stabling trains on a short term basis.

'SHUNT' AND 'SHED SHUNT' TURNS

The roster clerk began to place me on shunt duties once I had signed off Lover's Walk. 'Shed shunt' turns mostly involved staying within the depot boundaries. I would wait in the shunters lobby/signal cabin until the signaller required me to move units around the depot. A lot of time was spent, with a shunter, making up trains for the rush hours. Units also had to be moved into the shed for examinations or repair. Sometimes it was a simple case of propelling a unit through the washer and then running it back to where it came from. Propelling involved driving in reverse from the buffer stops end of a train. A shunter, who became your eyes and ears, sat in the rear cab and gave instructions via the loudaphone while operating the horn or emergency brake as and when required. On one occasion, I set back through the washer after being given permission to proceed by the shunter. As I propelled past the shunters' lobby I was dismayed to see that the shunter had jumped out of the train to have a chat with somebody down on the tarmac. This left me with no look out as I ran backwards through the washer with an eight car train!

There were three or four driver's diagrams per day which were completely composed of shunt duties. Running right through the day and night, the purpose of these duties was to move rolling stock between the station and depot. If you were unlucky, you would catch a duty that had been worked out with no logic whatsoever! You could end up walking quite a few miles if each movement came out of the depot to the station or vice versa. The carefully worked out duties saw a movement into the depot followed by a movement out of the depot, and so on ...

All of these duties came with the added incentive of earning your £10 D.O.O. money for the day. Driver restructuring eventually dispensed with D.O.O. and mileage payments (there was a bonus for driving more than two hundred miles in a day). Drivers went on to a set salary which incorporated these bonuses and made it a fairer system. The shed shunt turns also disappeared at this time. The shunters were trained to drive within the depot boundary so that main line drivers could be utilised more efficiently. This was a shame because shed shunt duties made a pleasant change from working on passenger trains. Station to depot moves were still carried out by main line drivers but were more often sandwiched between passenger workings. This mostly dispensed with the shunt duty diagrams.

OTHER ROUTES

Although occasionally landing a driving turn, the next few months were mostly spent sitting in the second man's seat with photocopied route plans on my lap. I learned the West Coastway down to Portsmouth, Littlehampton and Bognor Regis and this was followed by Eastbourne, Hastings and the line between Lewes and Keymer Junction which ran via Plumpton. I signed the main line as far as Haywards Heath as a relief driver but I quickly moved up into link four and signed the rest of the route to Victoria. I had already driven over the main line for many hours with my minder so I took a few excursions to satisfy my curiosity. I took a ride up to St. Albans in the cab of a 319 Thameslink unit. It was very interesting running through Borough Market and Metropolitan Junctions before descending down the amazing 1 in 29 gradient which led from Blackfriars to City Thameslink. I also managed a few trips on loco hauled services which included a few Gatwick Expresses and a class 47 on a cross-country service from East Croydon down to Brighton. It was interesting to see how differently locomotives rode at speed when compared with multiple units. I have to say that units won hands-down every time. The locos would rock and roll at the slightest ripple in the track! The smoothest cab ride that I ever managed was on a class 442 Wessex unit between Havant and Portsmouth Harbour. Commonly known among crews as 'plastic pigs', these units had extremely comfortable cabs and a riding quality that was more akin to gliding than running on rails.

Route learning could sometimes be enlightening. Drivers would point out interesting historical features of the line such as where nasty derailments or particularly gory suicides had taken place! There was a wonderful black sense of humour which helped train crews to deal with incidents that could seriously affect their working lives. The older drivers had the keenest knowledge and would relay facts such as why severe speed restrictions were put into place in certain locations. Bopeep tunnel, for instance, has a 30mph speed limit due to the fact that it is narrower than most other tunnels. The permanent way inside the tunnel was a little on the rough side and if a train was driven through too quickly there was a risk that it could roll a little and strike the tunnel walls. In the days of steam, and due to the tight confines, certain classes of engine were not allowed to pass each other within the tunnel. This was a favourite place for traction inspectors to use their speed guns, usually from the safety of Hastings station platform which looked straight along the bores of Hastings and Bopeep tunnels.

Many link four duties were based around the Coastway services which ran East and West out of Brighton. Portsmouth Harbour stopping services could drag if the guard held the train up at stations while selling tickets. A return trip could be gruelling work with the best part of four hours driving and sixty stops to make. Link four, as the junior men, usually got the scraps! That said,

Pompey stoppers, with a good guard, would fill half of your day's duty in one hit and could be quite relaxing once you got into the start/stop routine. The next station was often in sight before pulling away from the current one!

Making up time became quite a challenge, if starting out late from Portsmouth, with the last train of the day. With a four car unit you could just about get the time back by Hove. With good signalling, an efficient guard and a 3 COP unit, you could sometimes make up the time without breaking the speed limit before reaching Barnham. The 3 COP units, which had the same 1000hp as a four car unit, minus the 31-ton T.S.O, were quick off the mark when accelerating. A note about the performance of 3 COP units: I once worked a fast train formed with three 3 COP units between Victoria and Brighton. The ratio of three motor coaches to six trailer vehicles seemed to have a dramatic effect on acceleration. I was lucky enough to have good signals and managed to attain 90mph between Earlswood and Patcham tunnel, only slowing for the short 80mph speed restriction near Balcombe Tunnel Junction. I am sure that, given their head, the units would have attained well in excess of 100mph on the gentle downhill gradient from Balcombe, across the Ouse Valley Viaduct and on through Haywards Heath. I was careful to rein the units in and remembered my minder telling me that it was easy to let a train take control in such circumstances and that concentration and a firm hand was needed, particularly when on a downhill gradient. This was all very true. I arrived at Brighton five or six minutes early, no doubt due to the fact that I could attain any line speed very quickly over the entire course of the journey. I once heard some drivers mention that they had experienced going too fast on COP units without realising. They then had to use a lot of brake to decelerate or stop. The very same thing once happened to me when approaching Newhaven town in the down direction. It didn't occur a second time. Drivers always learned from their mistakes and never forgot a close run thing! There was a, sometimes noticeable, lack of brake force on these units, no doubt due to the lack of the trailer second vehicle and this would certainly have been the reason for heavier braking if a driver was caught out in such a situation. It is interesting to note that the 3 COPs were never given a lower speed restriction when the trailer seconds, and their very useful amount of brake force, were removed from the equation. The South Eastern's 3 CEP stock was restricted to a maximum speed of 75mph for this very reason. Link four contained most of the very early starts and very late finishes and included the first and last Pompey and the first and last Seaford workings. Most duties also contained very early or late runs between Brighton and Lover's Walk depot. The odd fast and semi-fast Victoria trains were in some diagrams but these were few and far between.

I learned more routes over the years as I progressed through the links. Link three brought knowledge of the Mid-Sussex line and in link two I learned the line from East Croydon to London Bridge which was to become my favourite stretch of track. Although short, this route was interesting because of the amount of routes which could be taken between New Cross Gate and London Bridge. The lines got busier and the signals were packed more and more tightly together as you approached the terminus. I also learned the route from Sydenham to Balham, via Crystal Palace and Streatham Hill. This was only ever traversed by Brighton drivers if there was engineering work or if empty coaching stock was being moved between Streatham Hill depot, London Bridge and Victoria.

LINKS

Electrification of the Brighton line was completed in 1933 and in the following year the Brighton branch of ASLEF was split into two separate depots. Enginemen and fireman belonged to Brighton number one branch while the motormen belonged to Brighton number two branch which also incorporated motormen from West Worthing depot.

Further expansion of electrification increased the need for more motormen and in time many enginemen and firemen transferred from branch number one to branch number two, which became one of the largest depots of motormen on the Southern Railway. Enginemen who had transferred to the motormen's depot were not permitted to return to the steam depot.

The two branches were amalgamated with the introduction of Thameslink services in 1988, for which more E.M.U. trained drivers were required, and a new system with four links was introduced. Prior to the amalgamation, Brighton number one depot consisted of two driver's links, plus a second man's link. Number two depot consisted of a link of motormen, plus a small medically restricted link that shunted trains between Lover's Walk depot and Brighton station.

The system, by dividing the drivers up into four sections or 'links', allowed drivers to gain experience gradually and helped to cut back on 'refreshers' which were required if a driver did not work over a particular route or drive a particular type of traction for six months. Keeping refreshers to a minimum meant that more drivers were available for driving turns. Movement up into the next link involved learning new routes and gaining more traction knowledge.

- Link one, the mixed traction link, a remnant of the original Brighton enginemen's depot, worked on 1963s, 319s, de-icing units and diesel locomotives.
- Link two, a remnant of the original Brighton motormen's depot, worked on 1963 stock, 319s and de-icing units. This link was originally for the senior motormen, who had been appointed prior to 1961, who did not wish to be trained on locomotives. The link should have got smaller as the older motormen retired but in time union intervention ensured that it developed into a progressive

link to bring it in line with the other three.

- Link three, also a remnant of the original motormen's depot, worked on 1963 stock and de-icing units.
- Link four worked on 1963 stock units only.

The basis of this system, although ever evolving, was still in use when I became a driver and each link had its own set of driving diagrams. The roster clerk would utilise the drivers and diagrams to the best advantage so that all train services were provided. Links were gained solely on a seniority basis. A driver with enough seniority from another depot could transfer into a vacant position. If not, each driver, with a vacancy above him, would move up towards the next link.

The tables below display the routes, including sidings, which were covered by each link at Brighton when I passed out as a driver. The separate Thameslink depot had not then opened so I have included the Brighton to Bedford route because links one and two covered this work. The E.C.S. runs to Fratton depot had ceased by this time so I have omitted Fratton from the list. I have also omitted the relief/starter link which drivers were placed in until they had signed the necessary routes to be placed into link four.

RUNNING LINES	Link 4	Link 3	Link 2	Link 1
Brighton to Victoria (including bi-directional lines between Preston Park & Balcombe)	*	*	*	*
East Croydon to London Bridge (Central)			*	*
Brighton to Bedford (via London Bridge South Eastern. Also via Elephant & Castle)			*	*
Falcon Junction (Clapham Junction) to Kensington Olympia				*
Sydenham / Norwood Junction to Balham (via Crystal Palace)			*	
Brighton to Eastbourne & Hastings (via Lewes)	*	*	*	*
Southerham Junction to Seaford	*	*	*	*
Lewes to Keymer Junction	*	*	*	*
Brighton to Portsmouth Harbour (including Littlehampton, Bognor Regis & the Cliftonville Spur)	*	*	*	*
Mid-Sussex Line, Arundel Junction to Three Bridges (via Horsham)		*	*	*
Brighton to Bournemouth (via Southampton inc. Eastleigh diversion)				*

DEPOTS, YARDS & SIDINGS	Link 4	Link 3	Link 2	Link 1
Brighton Lover's Walk depot & sidings	*	*	*	*
Three Bridges yard				*
Gatwick Airport sidings	*	*	*	*
Redhill yards				*
Selhurst depot & Norwood yard				*
Streatham Hill depot			*	
Victoria – Battersea Pier & Pugs Hole sidings	*	*	*	*
Lewes – Wall siding	*	*	*	*
Eastbourne sidings	*	*	*	*
Hastings – Park sidings	*	*	*	*
Hove yard				*
West Worthing carriage shed	*	*	*	*
Littlehampton shed & sidings	*	*	*	*
Barnham sidings	*	*	*	*
Bognor Regis sidings	*	*	*	*
Chichester yard				*
Eastleigh works				*
Horsham sidings		*	*	*

A day in the life ...

Drivers had to book on for duty in front of the train crew supervisor. The booking on time for the duty may have been altered and this would have been checked before leaving work on the previous shift. The weekly notices and late notice case had to be checked before leaving the booking-on point. These would display details of alterations to services, signalling and the locations of emergency speed restrictions. Occasionally, there would be a note pinned to the door which gave the location of speed-gun wielding traction inspectors! As mentioned above, speed limits were strictly adhered to but it was good to know the position of a speed trap. One mph above the 3mph grace could mean the difference between continuing with the journey or being taken off the track for re-assessment. A driver who had spotted a speed gun would warn other drivers by flashing the headlight or holding up one hand in the toy gun position as used when playing cowboys and Indians as a child!

As I settled into link four I began to get into the routine of driving on a day to day basis. The roster followed a pattern which involved working alternate weeks of 'earlies' and 'lates'. Early turns had booking-on times which started from midnight to midday and lates ran from midday to midnight. Drivers could work out mutual changeovers between themselves if duties conflicted with their personal lives. Favours could be returned at a later date and these, of course, had to be cleared with the roster clerk. A minimum break of twelve hours off was required between shifts.

The roster for each link would, for example, cover a period of thirty-six weeks and a driver would move down the roster, one line at a time, on a weekly basis. Each week was numbered and would display the number of hours worked, where the rest days fell, and which duties/diagrams were to be worked, including starting/finishing times, i.e. diagram 154, on 15.04, off 00.41, total 9 hours 37mins.

A driver's diagram sheet, or 'duty', contained the details of all trains to be driven on a shift. For each train, the sheet would display the train I.D. e.g. 2F15 which would be a class 2 passenger train to Seaford, the type of traction, times of station stops, junction passing times, head codes, and whether coaches were to be attached or detached en route. Some stations had various abbreviations placed next to their names, e.g. 'AP Haywards Heath'. This meant that the driver had to attach one portion of a train to another at Haywards Heath. The abbreviations found on Southern's driver's diagrams were as follows:

AP	attach portion
DP	detach portion
PA	portion attached (by another driver)
PD	Portion detached (by another driver)
PC	Prepare circuits (this generally meant that the train would already have been in service but the handbrake may have been applied)
TC	Trip circuits (the handbrake would need to be applied if the train was due to stand idle for some time)
PB	Prepare from berth (prepare the train for service, 'cut in' if necessary)
B	Berth (switch the lights off and apply the handbrake, 'cut out' if necessary)
RA	Relieved at (relieved by another driver on route)
RW	Relieve and work (relieve another driver on route)
ECS	Empty coaching stock
Pass	Ride as a passenger (e.g. back to home depot or to the next working)
Pass cab	as above but driver to ride in the cab to aid retention of route knowledge
PNB	Personal needs break
SO	Saturdays only
SX	Saturdays excepted
SUN	Sundays only
400 series	Type of traction to be worked (400 series – 1963 stock)
319	Type of traction to be worked (class 319)
377	Type of traction to be worked (class 377)

Listed below are some basic examples of diagrams which I worked on during the course of my progression to link two:

Early turn: Brighton to Seaford (semi-fast staff train)
(Mon to Fri) Seaford to Brighton (stopping service)
Brighton to Eastbourne (stopping service)
PNB
Eastbourne to Littlehampton (via platform 3 Brighton, stopping service)
ECS, shunt to wash train if required
Littlehampton to Brighton (stopping service)
This turn was commonly known as the 'First Seaford'
Early turn: ECS Lover's Walk depot to Brighton
(Mon to Fri) Brighton to Portsmouth Harbour and return (stopping)

PNB

Brighton to West Worthing and return (stopping service)

This turn was commonly known as the 'First Pompey'

Late turn: Brighton to Portsmouth Harbour (stopping service)

(Mon to Fri) Portsmouth Harbour to Barnham (stopping service)

Barnham to Bognor Regis (pass)

PNB

Bognor Regis to Three Bridges (stopping service, last train up the Mid-Sussex)

Three Bridges to Brighton (call at Haywards Heath only)

Late turn: ECS Lover's Walk depot to Brighton

(Mon to Fri) Brighton to Victoria and return (semi-fast)

Brighton to Victoria and return to Gatwick Airport (semi-fast)

PNB

Gatwick Airport to Victoria (semi-fast)

Victoria to Worthing (semi-fast)

ECS Worthing to Brighton

ECS Brighton to Lover's Walk depot

Late turn: ECS Lover's Walk to Victoria via Norwood Junction and

(Mon to Fri) Crystal Palace

Victoria to Littlehampton (semi-fast)

PNB

Littlehampton to Brighton (stopping service)

Brighton to Hove and return (Hove shuttle)

Night turn: Brighton to Victoria (semi-fast, last train to London from

(Mon to Fri) Brighton)

PNB

Victoria to Three Bridges and return (semi-fast)

Victoria to Brighton (semi-fast, first train to Brighton from London)

This turn was commonly known as the 'Night Gatwicks'

Early turn: Brighton to Victoria and return (fast)

(Sat only) PNB

Brighton to Victoria and return (fast)

Brighton to Victoria and return (fast)

PNB

Brighton to Seaford and return (stopping service)

Early turn: Brighton to Portsmouth Harbour and return (stopping

(Sun only) service)

PNB

Brighton to Hove and return (Hove shuttle)

Brighton to Portsmouth Harbour and return (stopping service)

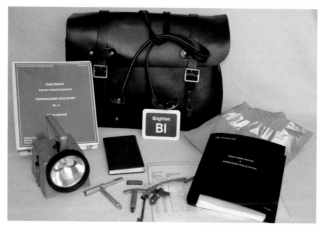

Driver's equipment. The leather driver's bag would contain train crew manuals, a Bardic hand lamp, diary, roster, spare keys, and a high visibility vest. It was not essential to carry the heavy rule book because a driver was expected to know it from memory. *Author*

Examples of 'BR 33056' train crew manuals which were carried by drivers at all times. *Author's collection*

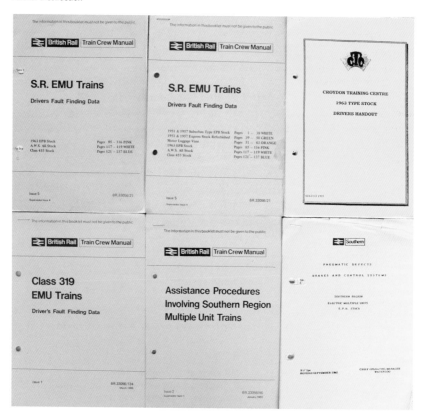

Drivers would occasionally be rostered to go on 'safety day' training courses. The safety briefings were given by traction inspectors who would inform drivers of new procedures and safe working practices. Many of the discussions were related to train protection, e.g. the use of track circuit operating clips and detonators in the event of an emergency where contact with the signalman was not possible. Use of the driver's reminder appliance (D.R.A.) was normally discussed and habitual use of this piece of equipment helped drivers to avoid passing signals at danger (S.P.A.D.s). At the end of the day we were asked if we had any concerns or ideas which may help to make the job run more smoothly. Railtrack required drivers to use the phonetic alphabet when contacting signalmen via the cab radio. All train identification numbers were supposed to be given using this form of pronunciation, i.e. 2F52 would become 'two foxtrot fifty-two.' The system had been put into place to help avoid signalling errors. 2F52 could easily be misheard as 2S52 over the radio. A lot of drivers were not using the phonetic alphabet and an inspector, on one of the safety days, gave us a hard talking to on the subject. I suggested that it may help drivers to learn more easily if a sticker displaying the phonetic alphabet was placed, on the wall, next to the cab radio. The traction inspector's face lit up and stickers began to appear in the cabs within a week. From then on, I used the stickers when calling the signalmen and learned the phonetic alphabet without realising it!

All drivers had to take an annual rules examination with a traction inspector. The length of the exam would generally depend on how well a driver performed under pressure. Books would be checked, to make sure that they were up to date and questioning on the finer points of the rule book could last for quite some time if the inspector was a stickler. The day usually ended with a trip to Lover's Walk where the inspector would go over some traction knowledge whilst looking over a unit. The rules day could be mentally exhausting but it served as a refresher and helped to keep a driver up to date with regulations which constantly evolved as safety standards improved. All inspectors were ex-drivers and most were firm but fair. Drivers rarely failed their exam. Only rarely would an inspector become 'poacher turned game-keeper' and try to make a name for themselves. A driving licence and personal track safety card had to be carried at all times. These would be re-issued, if necessary, at the end of the annual rules test.

Connex South Central driving licence and. safety critical I.D. card

A traction inspector would regularly ride with new drivers during their first couple of years. As time passed, the rides would get fewer and further between and in the end would become a yearly assessment. Inspectors normally rode in the front cab but could also ride in the train or rear cab, where they would monitor the speedometer and brake gauges. It was always considered to be unfair and rather devious, to monitor a driver from the rear cab without their prior knowledge! Usually, the traction inspector would chat or go over the use of new equipment such as the D.R.A. The inspector would issue the driver with an assessment feedback form at the end of the ride.

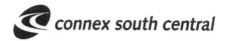

ASSESSMENT FEEDBACK

DRIVER: T WOOD

ASSESSOR: M D STYLES

DATE: 14.04.98

Following your 7th Post Assessment on the above date. You drove to a high standard.

Areas discussed were:-

> Driver Reminder appliance.
>
> Cab proceedure to prevent starting against a signal at danger.

Very good performance, with no areas of concern.

This assessment covers unit 2.3, 3.1, 3.2, 3.3

Driver signature........T...S..Wood.....

Assessor signature...M.D..style..............

Driver's assessment feedback form. The form was issued by my traction inspector after completing a return trip to Portsmouth Harbour. *Author's collection*

Classes 319 and 377

I was required to drive class 319 units upon entering link two. A two week traction conversion course at Brighton was followed by a few days of practical handling on the main line. Sixty dual-voltage 319 units were originally built for use on the Brighton to Bedford 'Thameslink' services where current collection changed from the third rail dc supply to the overhead ac supply at Farringdon. It was found that only forty units were required for the Thameslink work and so twenty were transferred to Selhurst depot for utilisation on the Central where they replaced the last remaining EPB units. These units became indispensable on the Central and so more 319s were built for Thameslink as the Brighton to Bedford work increased over time. Seven of the Central units were later converted for use on the 'Connex Express' services which released the 'Capital Coast Express' 8 DIGs back into normal service as four car units. The 319s had a good rate of acceleration and were even faster when driven on the ac supply under the wires.

The power and brake handles were much simpler to use than those fitted to '63 stock. The power handle had four notches which increased the power by 25% with each notch. The three-step Westcode brake handle had three 'service' positions with the addition of 'emergency' if required. The units were fitted with a foot pedal operated D.S.D./vigilance device and wheel slip detection which made things easier for the driver with regards to accelerating and braking on poor rail head conditions. 319s were certainly prone to slipping and sliding on the slightest amount of moisture. The disc braking system, although capable of smooth and comfortable operation, did not have the adjustability of the E.P. brake or the fierceness of that fitted to the class 377 units which usually felt like an anchor had been thrown on to the track!

When the course was complete I took a driving test with my traction inspector. There were two of us to be passed out and I volunteered to take the controls when we were asked who wanted to go first. By this time, driver only operation (D.O.O.) had been cleared for the entire Brighton mainline but it was not allowed if the train was formed with more than eight coaches. The train, luckily for me, was formed with twelve which meant that a guard worked the sliding doors, leaving me to concentrate on the driving only. The train was an early morning commuter service to London Bridge and my trip ran on time right into the terminus. We detached one unit on arrival and the

Having worked down the main line from Watford Junction, 319 012 approaches platform 5 at Brighton, 22nd April 2005. *Author*

other man worked the train back to Brighton as a semi-fast service. He, of course, had to deal with the operation of the doors in addition to driving. These units were easy to drive and we both passed our tests without mishap.

Most of the 319 work was carried out on fast Brighton to Victoria services with the occasional Watford Junction thrown in for good measure. Brighton men only took these services as far as East Croydon or Selhurst where they were relieved by a Norwood driver who would take the train on to Watford. These runs were more interesting than the fasts because they were booked to stop at more stations. Accuracy when stopping was imperative because the cab had to line up with D.O.O. monitors and mirrors on the station platforms. 'Right Away' indicators were provided at the bigger stations so that platform staff could let the driver know when it was all clear to start. I became fond of the 319s because, at the time, they made quite a change to driving '63 stock which was still the staple traction for the lion's share of Brighton turns.

The 319s were good units but there were a few points that I was not enamoured with as a driver. The first was not so much the units themselves but the way in which they were operated. The driver had to make public address announcements because there was no guard on D.O.O. services. This was necessary but not always convenient if things were busy in the cab such as when driving in poor visibility or when running under cautionary signals towards a terminus. I have always believed that there should be a guard on every train. Passengers on D.O.O. services could not always get the information they required and more importantly, the guard was a great necessity should something untoward happen, especially if the driver became incapacitated. Secondly, some units had very draughty emergency doors on the unit ends. At best, these could be noisy, particularly in tunnels. At worst, they would make the cab freezing in the winter! I am sure this could have been remedied with a little thought and investment. Lastly, I had a personal gripe with a particular unit. 319 217 had a reputation with drivers as being unreliable and prone to failure. It always behaved impeccably for me but 216 didn't seem to like me! On one occasion the unit shut down, for no apparent reason, when driving at high speed. All power was lost and the brakes carried out an emergency stop just to the north side of Gatwick Airport. I had only been driving the units for a month or so at this time and it was not a pleasant experience for me or the passengers! I did what I was taught to do by other drivers when this sort of incident occurred. I took my key off and put it on again. It worked and the unit was fine for the rest of the journey! Unfortunately, it died again, just a few weeks later, when I stopped at Three Bridges station. I opened up the power handle to pull away and nothing happened. I shut off and tried again but to no avail so I took my key off and re-applied it. She took off as if nothing had happened and then proceeded to carry out a repeat performance when I stopped at another station. I reported

My 'Nemesis' unit. 319 216 awaits the road at Brighton, 22nd April 2005. *Author*

the erratic behaviour on both occasions but the fitters could find no problems. From then on, I got a sinking feeling whenever I saw 216 roll into Brighton ready for my next working. Intermittent faults were rare but certainly did not inspire confidence when alone and driving at high speed with a train full of passengers! I asked around but nobody else seemed to have had any trouble with the unit. I do not recall further problems but my mistrust had been well established and so I always drove 216 with a feeling of doubt!

The death knell of slam door rolling stock rang out when the first class 375/3 units arrived at Brighton. The units quickly became class 377/3 when the couplings were changed from tightlock to Dellner. Most of the drivers at the depot were wary of what the future might hold. It must be remembered that the slam door stock had provided a very reliable service and 1963 stock driving cabs had been a Southern Region driver's second home for a very long time. I was rostered on to a two-week traction conversion course fairly soon after the first 377s had arrived at Lover's Walk. The first week of the course saw me and other apprehensive drivers being shown around the new units, learning what traction knowledge we could on the way. The instructors were not very familiar with the units and when asked, could not inform me where the motor bogies were to be found! "You won't need to know where they are, there is very little that you can do if one of these things goes wrong, just phone a fitter!" came the reply. This did not instil confidence for the future! We learned how to prepare a unit and luckily there were two in the depot so we had a go at coupling and uncoupling the pair. It took six attempts to make a good connection between the units because the MITRAC computers, one fitted in each unit, would not communicate with each other! Once the attachment was complete it took quite some time before the computer screen showed that both units were up and running in unison. This problem occurred for quite some time after the units had entered service and for a while, units with differing computer programs could not be attached to each other! We then covered brake faults with their appropriate procedures and isolations were looked at in some detail. There was a panel on the right hand side of the cabs which contained a lot of switches. These were mostly for carrying out isolations, such as for AWS and TPWS faults. The doors could be controlled by using the touch sensitive MITRAC computer screen and exterior headlights and marker lights had a circuit proving LED display so the driver no longer had to get out of the cab and check the front of the train before beginning a journey. This certainly was an advantage and the units had many up to date features such as air conditioning and a passenger address system. The passenger address could be operated by both driver and guard but there were problems with the system for quite some time. On approach to a station, the system would often announce the wrong station name. It could sometimes be a station which was not on the line that the unit was travelling over! The toilets were another early problem. The electronic

South Central

Class 375/377

Drivers Update
Issue No 1

The front cover of the first issue of the Southern class 375/377 train crew manual showed a rather elongated version of a class 375. *Author's collection*

sliding doors would lock once the tank was about two thirds full and there were reports of people getting locked in. This did not go down well with the travelling public and many services were run with no toilets from beginning to end.

We spent a week working empty trains, with a driving instructor, between Brighton and Eastbourne. The combined brake/power handle was quite something to get used to and a notice had been issued which stated that the 'hill start' button was to be used at all times when pulling away. If a unit rolled back slightly, with the master switch in 'forward', the computer would get confused and shut the unit down! The power circuits would take about five seconds to come in when taking power so the hill start button was used to hold the brake 'on' until the motors began to pull. The five second delay was caused when the combined handle was moved from 'brake' through 'neutral' and into 'power'. The hill start button cured the problem but it was simpler to hold the brake with one hand and the power handle with the other as on the older units.

With three service positions, the brakes were very powerful when compared with 319s. Step one was only considered to be a 'holding still' brake on 319s. It was quite fierce on 377s and I never used more than step two when driving in service or on empty stock workings. The instructor asked me to demonstrate the emergency brake whilst running at 80mph on the approach to Glynde. The unit stopped in an incredibly short distance. The braking was certainly an advance in technology but it was not an advance in comfort. The ride took a little getting used to as well. When in training, I was sitting at the back of a unit and experienced travel sickness for the first time on a train. This did not seem to occur when driving but quite a few guards took travel sickness pills for some time after the units were put into public service.

I passed my 377 conversion course and spent an apprehensive Christmas dreading my first turn out on the track with one. There was a lot of new technology to get to grips with. Sure enough, somebody pulled a passenger communication handle at Moulsecoomb, seven minutes into my first trip, which happened to be a Seaford service on New Year's Day! There was an over-ride fitted to the pass-comm system so I managed to get into the

377 406 in platform five at Lewes, 6th November 2012. *Author*

platform before stopping. The MITRAC screen showed me where the handle had been pulled and I went back to re-set it. It had been pulled by a young man who was a little the worse for wear from the previous night! The override button was a good advancement. Trains could no longer be stopped in tunnels or opposite the homes of mischievous youths.

Most of these problems were gradually ironed out although there were still details that were badly designed. An air conditioning vent blew hot or cold air directly down on to the driver's head! The driver's seat was too far back from the windscreen so it gave the driver a very narrow field of vision. The traction inspectors said that this would keep us from going too close to red signals because you had to stop further back from them to be able to see them. This theory was not compatible with the tight track circuit sections and overhead signal gantries to be found at East Croydon and London Bridge. There was a high/small cab side window which was of no use at all. The driver's door had an opening window but you had to get up and walk behind the driver's seat to open it. This was inconvenient when communicating with a member of platform staff or with a shunter down on the track. The passenger information system could clearly be heard in the driving cab and was a real nuisance when on the radio to a signalman.

Design faults aside, the 377s settled down into service. The crews and travelling public gradually got used to them although sitting on hard seats that were not designed to line up with windows offered a poor second to the plush cushioning of Mark I rolling stock. Reliability seems to be the only concern and with many years ahead of them, the 377s have got a lot to live up to. They will do well if they can manage half of the work carried out by 1963 stock units, some of which had three million miles on the clock when they were hauled away for disposal.

12

Out on the track

The day to day routine of being a train driver can, in some respects, be compared to working in any other profession because most work is based on repetition. Although I enjoyed driving trains, most days were uneventful and were forgotten by the time I arrived home. This is a perfectly normal way of life for millions of people across the employment spectrum. I could not begin to count the amount of return runs which I completed on Brighton to London Victoria services alone. A collective wealth of knowledge and experience, which could only be gained over many years, was handed down to me from the more senior Brighton men, not forgetting of course, the invaluable time that I spent out on the track with my driving instructor. Many of the older men who worked at the depot are now retired. Train drivers of old would relish the status that came with the job and it was considered to be a job for life once they had reached the position. The turnover of drivers is much higher in this modern age because time and budgetary constraints have had their effect in the age of privatisation. The four hundred hours which I spent in training with my minder driver have been cut and raw recruits are now expected to learn in two hundred hours. Modern train drivers no longer have to get to grips with the Westinghouse automatic brake but the job should always demand a lengthy training period. Learning to drive hundreds of tons of steel, at high speed with many hundreds of passengers on board, should not be rushed. Driving trains is not for the faint hearted when in poor weather conditions. Line speed is adhered to wherever possible, even if it is raining, foggy and in pitch black darkness.

I came to relish challenging scenarios because they made a change from the norm. I would not like to have faced them with only half of the amount of experience in the cab. I can well remember the adrenaline flowing on many occasions and this made the job very memorable. Driving in heavy snowfall, where the muffled sound of the train running along the rails was eerily quiet, whilst the night sky was lit with heavy arcing, was to say the least, magical! I was based at Brighton for ten years, 1994 to 2004. The days that stand out are the ones which contained something really interesting, really good or really bad. I was lucky in a lot of respects in that nothing *really* bad happened to me but there were quite a few interesting incidents and close shaves which occurred over the years.

A DAY TO REMEMBER

I had a turn that seemed as though it would never end roughly six months after I had signed the road to London Bridge. The alarm woke me at about 4.45am and after a quick wash I stumbled out to the car for the ten-mile drive to Brighton. I had the radio on and the weather forecast stated that the prolonged hot spell was going to continue. I made a decision there and then to cut the grass when I got home and then put my feet up for an hour before collecting my son from school. As I trudged from the station car park, up to the signing on point, I wondered whether the turn was going to work out well for the plans that I had made for later on in the day. The latter part of the turn could go a matter of two ways. An empty stock working from Streatham Hill to Lover's Walk Depot meant I wouldn't get the gardening done. 'No empties required' meant ride 'pass' back to Brighton, head home early and enjoy the sunshine.

It was quiet on arrival at the signing on point. As per usual, a few drivers were lurking around in the lobby, waiting for the 'nod' from the train crew supervisor which would allow them to go home to bed after spending the night on shunt or spare duties. Most carried that expectant look, waiting for their relief comrades to arrive on time for their own turns. Night turn drivers often got away a little early if the T.C.S. was feeling charitable and nobody had phoned in sick. After checking the daily alterations, which showed nothing untoward, I grabbed a coffee and headed down to platform four for my first train of the day which was the 05.49 semi-fast to London Bridge.

The train was formed with two 4 VEPs. This was the usual formation because the train needed plenty of doors for eager commuters to scramble into. The train was booked to stop at all stations to Purley, then East Croydon, and finally ended with a run up the fast line to London Bridge. I entered the rear cab to wind off the handbrake and then made my way up the train chatting to the guard, us both agreeing to carry out a brake test when all was made ready. Whilst preparing the front cab I noticed another four car unit running in to platform four on top of my train. I presumed that something was running late or that there had been a signalling error, which was not unknown! I was about to call up Three Bridges box on the cab radio when a member of platform staff climbed into the cab and informed me that a preceding London Bridge service had been cancelled so another four coaches were being added to my train. The driver who brought in the CIG from Lover's Walk took care of the attachment so I again made my way to the front of the train. I can remember thinking "It's going to be one of those days!" knowing full well that this was always an extremely well loaded service and was now going to have a late start. London Bridge commuters were always known for making a point of looking at their watches in view of a driver as the train ran into a platform. With the preceding service cancelled, there would be more disgruntled faces than usual. I prepared the cab, wound the roller blinds to the number '15' headcode and buzzed the guard on the loudaphone for a brake test. This being satisfactory we pulled away from Brighton with a five minute late start.

The first few stops were fairly quiet and we made good progress. More people were beginning to appear as we ran into Burgess Hill and the first watch was held out, for me to see, on a long pinstriped arm. There were only a few passengers at Wivelsfield but the next stop, at Haywards Heath, was very busy and we left there seven minutes down. The sun was bright in the east and the day was warming up nicely. I had the cab window open on the run to Balcombe and there was a lovely view from the Ouse Valley viaduct. The tree tops below were poking out of a veil of mist which would soon burn off to brighten this tranquil scene. We were put on to the 'up slow' line at Balcombe Tunnel Junction and arrived at Three Bridges to find a packed platform with a few more watches on show. Gatwick Airport provided the usual struggle of tired holiday-makers, all trying to squeeze into the train with children and luggage. The platform staff gave us the 'right away' and we departed ten minutes late!

Horley, Salfords and Earlswood brought a steady string of people, all looking for seats which were beginning to run out. I could see through the vestibule behind my cab that people were already standing. As I ran through the 15mph crossovers and into Redhill I could see that platform two was packed to the edges. The starter signal was displaying a red aspect and after a few minutes, an 'up' Gatwick Express charged through the middle road and disappeared around the curve towards Merstham. We got the signal to proceed when the section cleared and I looked back to see if the doors were all shut. I was astounded to see that platform two was now empty! Carrying lots of weight was not often noticeable but the train needed more air in the brake cylinders than was normal when running into the next few stations.

The train was full to the brim before Purley. Now running fifteen minutes late, we crossed on to the 'up fast' line just north of Purley. At this point I was beginning to dread what East Croydon would bring. The platform was heaving and very few people managed to get on to the train. There was some shouting and there were a lot of grumbling voices. I kept my cab window shut tight until the guard rang two on the bell to proceed. The platform was still packed when we pulled away and I breathed a sigh of relief. There were no more stops to pick up at before reaching London Bridge.

The signal at Windmill Bridge Junction directed us on to the 'up fast London Bridge' line and I opened up the power handle with green signals as far as the eye could see. The train took a little longer than usual to attain the 70mph line speed after passing through Norwood Junction. From there, the line climbed steadily towards Forest Hill where the power was shut off as the train went over the visible summit. With the train now on a falling gradient,

I had the brakes rubbing firmly as we ran through Honor Oak Park. The front bogie dropped into a 'sump' when adjacent to the platforms. The sump was a wet spot in the ballast where the track had visibly dropped for about six feet in length. When sumps became too unsafe they were dug out until dry soil was reached. They were then refilled and the track was re-bedded. The bogie came back up with an almighty bang and for the first time I experienced the unnerving feeling of the suspension 'bottoming out'.

There must have been a heavy load in the leading driving trailer and I would have been able to see just how many people were crammed in had I been driving a VEP. By looking back through the windows in the two, centrally located, bulkhead doors which separated the driving cab from the passenger accommodation, the driver could get a rough idea of how many people were on board. This feature could be useful at times and allowed a driver to judge the behaviour of rowdy youths or football fans. A driver could not do this on CIGs or BIGs because the door between the cab vestibule and the passenger accommodation was at the side of the vehicle. VEPs could sometimes be a curse due to the large amount of passenger doors that were fitted. They were good for getting lots of people on board quickly but they could be a real nuisance if just one of those passengers did not close a door properly. The guard could be seen, frantically running up and down the length of the train, closing doors which were left 'on the catch' and time could be lost if this happened regularly on a stopping service, especially if the train was formed with three VEPs! I think most drivers, including myself, helped out by closing a door if it was not too far from the driving cab. Occasionally, when on the move, the signalman would have to be informed if an offside door was spotted 'on the catch'. The offender was often a VEP because of the amount of doors and the law of averages!

I applied more brake and looked back out of the cab window, hoping that the train would stay on the road. Luckily all looked well as we continued down Brockley Bank. The gradient was at its steepest here and I had to brake hard for the 60mph restriction on approach to New Cross Gate. I managed to get down to the correct speed halfway along the platform where I began to pick up double yellow signal aspects for the approach to Bricklayer's Arms Junction. I was pleased to be away from Brockley Bank because the train would have taken a lot of stopping if the signals had been against us on the gradient. This was, without doubt, the heaviest train that I had ever worked. I contacted London Bridge signal box and informed them of the poor ride through Honor Oak Park.

We pottered into London Bridge sixteen minutes late. T.P.W.S. had recently been fitted along the platforms so I crept up to the buffer stops at 6mph. Most of the passengers were off the train before I brought it to a gentle stand. T.P.W.S, when fitted to slam door trains with no central locking, was always a bad concoction. Commuters soon learned that it was quicker to jump off and hurry on foot to the ticket barriers. The brakes would have been applied automatically if the train had exceeded 6mph over the T.P.W.S. grid. This was the standard speed setting when on approach to buffers in dead-end platforms or bays.

I had no time for another coffee because I only had a ten minute turn round before running the train empty to Streatham Hill depot. I was already behind the schedule. The guard walked past me, looking fairly distressed, as I changed ends. I can only imagine the complaints that he must have had from the passengers! Overcrowding was a common problem on Southern Region lines at peak times.

The platform staff walked along the length of the train and closed the doors and windows because I was booked to run through the washer at Streatham Hill. Normally this was done by the depot shunter but he had phoned London Bridge and requested platform staff to help out. There was a queue of units gradually making their way through the wash and then back into the shed so things were getting behind at the depot. I pulled away from London Bridge twelve minutes late, having received the tip from the platform staff and the 'right away' indicator on the signal. There were stop marks on the sleepers, which the drivers had to pull up to, in front of the buffers at London Bridge. Normally, stopping six feet short was the requirement at terminus stations. The platform track circuits at 'The Bridge' were a little tight for length. If a twelve-car was not pulled right up to the stop board it would overhang the track circuit at the rear. This would not let the signalmen set other routes at the station throat. The starting signals, on the gantries above, could be quite hard to see because they were almost directly above the cab window.

The short run on empties was driver only operated and was booked to run via the fast line to Forest Hill where the crossover to the slow line was taken before coming off on the spur at Sydenham. The spur led round to Crystal Palace and then on to Streatham Hill. The signalman put me on to the slow line at Bricklayer's Arms Junction. I opened up the power handle, in order to gain speed for the run up Brockley Bank, as I ran through New Cross Gate. The train got up to about 50mph when, to my horror, there was an uncontrolled emergency brake application. This could normally be put down to somebody pulling the emergency cord on a passenger train but on an empty stock working all sorts of horrible scenarios began to run through my mind. Train divided, burst brake pipe, derailment! I looked back out of my side window as the train slowed. All looked well but I thought that my gardening plans were probably going to be cancelled as the train came to a grinding halt.

I called London Bridge signal box to explain that I was going to look around the train to see if I could find the problem. The weather was hot and, with all of the windows closed; the interior of the train was like a furnace as

4 CIG 1753 (Originally built as 7327) stands in Platform eleven at London Bridge, 2nd May 1994. Central section trains used the terminus platforms, eight to sixteen, while Eastern section services traversed the high level 'through' platforms. *Ashley Barton*

if I wasn't in a sweat anyway! Upon approaching the rear of the train I was beginning to think that I would have to walk back to the front in the cess, looking along the outside for broken pipes. It was lucky that I was not on the fast line as booked. The fast London Bridge lines ran in between the slow lines, a fairly unusual feature on the Central.

I finally made it to the rear coach only to find a rather large lady sitting in the very last compartment of the CIG unit. The passenger communication cord was dangling on the wall above her. The London Bridge staff must have missed her boarding the train and she somehow thought that the train was calling at New Cross Gate! I persuaded the lady to walk to the front and explained that I would have to drop her off at the next station. Brockley was unmanned and so I would have to see myself away from the platform. I leaned out of the coach to reset the communication cord with the butterfly. It took nearly ten minutes to walk the lady to the front of the train, by which time she was fairly breathless and was suffering from the heat. I called the signalman again to explain the situation. He asked me to fill out a report form before going off duty.

I recharged the brake pipe and continued on to Brockley where I pulled the front cab to just past the north end platform ramp. This avoided stopping the train next to the busy platform; I didn't want any more uninvited passengers boarding the train as I pulled away. The exhausted lady disembarking caused some amusement for the spectators on the station. I wished her a good day and applied some power. The rest of the journey went smoothly and the washer was available for a clear run on arrival at Streatham Hill. I had given all of the other trains plenty of time to get out of the way! When asked, the shunter informed me that he didn't know if the empties were running back to Lover's Walk. If they were, I would face a two hour break at Streatham followed by a long slow run down to Brighton because class five empty trains were put behind any passenger workings. I pulled the train into the shed and applied the handbrake before making my way to the nearest phone where I called Control. "Hello Control. Driver of the Streatham to Lover's empties here, anything to go down to Brighton?" "Not today mate, can we have a copy of your report form before you go home?"

I jumped on the first train to Clapham Junction and from there got the fastest train that I could find down to the coast. Luckily that trip went well and I got the report form filled out on the way. On arrival at Brighton, the train crew supervisor had a quick look at the form; "Uncontrolled brake application with nobody on board! Bet you s*** yourself!" I told him that it had not been a day that I wanted to repeat in a hurry. Against all the odds, I got home in time to cut the grass but before I started I sat down to have something to eat and promptly fell asleep on the sofa. When I awoke I had to rush to collect my son from school. I was 'rest day off' on the next day and so I did eventually get the grass cut!

This incident certainly pointed out the disadvantages of slam door units when compared with modern rolling stock. The MITRAC screen in the cab of a class 377 displayed all of the information that a driver needed, including the location of a problem and how to remedy it so no physical search of the train was required. The centrally locked doors could not be used by passengers unless the driver allowed them to be opened. It was not unknown for passengers to be found climbing out of a slam door train that had just been berthed in sidings!

Streatham Hill carriage sheds carried none of the complexity of Lover's Walk depot. The conductor rails stopped at the entrance to the sheds and so the rear driving trailer had to be left, just outside, to keep a collector shoe 'on the juice'. It was best to get to the depot early if a twelve car train needed to be prepared for service. The compressors on the unit in contact with the conductor rail could take quite some time to pump up the whole of the train. Occasionally, on summer Saturdays, Brighton crews would work empty twelve car trains to Streatham Hill sheds for what was known as 'hand bashing'. Cleaners would scrub the outside of the units with brooms and strong chemicals and when their work was finished, the driver would run the train through the carriage washer to give the units a rinse. There was a grumpy old chap whose job was to set the points and start the washer running once a train had been pulled up to his cabin. I was waiting for another train to clear the washer on a bright summer's morning and the old boy was sitting in a deck chair, next to the washer control buttons, with a newspaper on his lap. It being a nice day, there was a robin singing its little heart out in one of the trees above him. I remember the man looking up and telling the cheery little bird to shut the **** up, you ****! This man really did not know which side his bread was buttered on. He probably had the easiest and most pleasant job on the entire network!

FAULTS AND FAILURES

Most of the faults and failures which occurred whilst I was driving at Brighton happened on 1963 stock. This makes sense because I spent most of my time driving them, with only the last few years combining '63s with 319s and 377s. Putting the minor faults aside, such as changing a fuse, I have included all of the more serious faults that I experienced with '63 stock over the ten year period. There are only six listed, which just goes to show how reliable these units were, especially considering that they were driven into the ground on a daily basis for forty or so years. Credit must be given to the maintenance staff who diligently kept the units running in good order right to the end of their working lives.

The first fault in service occurred whilst working a semi-fast train from Littlehampton to Victoria via Hove. It was a cold winter's evening and there was a layer of snow on the ground. The unit was a 4 CIG and having completed a successful brake test with the guard, we departed Littlehampton and headed towards Arundel Junction. The unit behaved normally until I braked for the first stop at Angmering where I discovered that I could only make a full service brake application. The brake cylinders filled to 50lb/psi as soon as I moved the brake handle away from the release position. This caused the unit to stand on its nose but I managed to stop, rather abruptly, somewhere near to the four car mark. The guard didn't seem to notice and I tried the first trick in the book which was always carried out if a brake fault was suspected. I 'blew the brake out' which involved smartly putting the brake handle to the emergency position so as to drain the brake pipe quickly. This procedure would normally have cleared a brake fault, or dragging brake, nine times out of ten. I allowed the pipe to recharge and proceeded towards the next stop at Goring where I braked early but the same thing happened again. I managed to stop near the four car mark by placing the brake handle to 'apply' and then quickly back to 'release' without letting the brake cylinders have more than about 20lb/psi. It was a shaky stop but it was smoother than the one at Angmering. I blew the brake out again but to no avail so I carefully made my way to Worthing which was only a couple of stops further on. I attempted to use the autobrake but I could still only get a full service application. The passengers were de-trained at Worthing and I was instructed to get the unit to Hove where another driver would be waiting with a replacement unit for me to take up the main line. He would take the faulty one into Lover's Walk depot for the fitters to look at. I explained the fault to him on arrival at Hove and wished him luck as he pulled away. I waited for my passengers to catch up on the following Brighton service and then proceeded on to London Victoria. I managed to speak to the fitters on the following day. When on test, the unit had behaved in the same way for a short time and then the fault had cleared by itself. The fitters could only come up with one explanation which was that there may have been some ice in the main reservoir pipe. Compressed air can make water condense. If this had happened, it could easily have frozen in the pipe, causing the brakes to behave erratically. The carriage sheds were always warm in the winter and this would explain why the fault had cured itself. Soon after this, all units were fitted with what was known as a 'spit valve' on the main reservoir pipe. These were placed at a low point in the system where water would accumulate. It would then literally be spat out, at intervals, so as to keep the pipe clear of moisture.

The next fault that I was involved with occurred when relieving an Eastbourne driver at Victoria. He had just worked a twelve car train into the station and on arrival he explained to me that the train had felt very 'snatchy' when pulling away and braking. He closed his cab down and made sure that the brakes were in 'full service' before we walked along the train looking for a possible problem. The fault soon showed itself. There were no brake blocks in contact with the wheels on the motor coach of the 4 BIG which was situated in the centre of the train. It was no wonder that the train had felt rough on the inward journey! The motor coach was completely unbraked and was one of the heaviest vehicles in the train. Un-braked vehicles on the railway were known as 'swingers' for obvious reasons! I did not find out what had caused the fault but I only took the top four coaches down to Eastbourne which left the BIG and another CIG stranded in platform seventeen during the rush hour at Victoria!

I only came across one more serious brake fault and this occurred when preparing a 4 CIG in platform two at Brighton. For a short time, a four coach service went up to Victoria via West Worthing. On arrival at Haywards Heath, the train would be attached to the rear of an up Eastbourne service before continuing on to London. The unit was 'flat' when I put my key on but had only been in the station for about twenty minutes. The main reservoir took about five minutes to charge as opposed to the usual two minutes. It then took a long time before I could charge the brake pipe to release the brakes. I tested the E.P. brake which did not respond very well at all. Out of interest, I tested the autobrake which worked but took much too long to recharge. By this time, the autobrake had been banned from use when working on passenger trains and should only have been used on empty stock workings to keep a driver's hand in.

4 VEP 3514 (originally built as unit 7837) in perfect working order at Brighton! The 'white blanks' headcode gives away the fact that the unit is about to be worked from platform two into Lover's Walk depot via the west carriage road. 22nd April 2005. *Author*

With some justification, I refused to work the train. I was then handed a phone by a member of the platform staff and was informed that a top manager, who was in London at the time, would like to speak to me. I do not know how he found out what was going on so quickly but he asked me what was wrong with the unit and I explained the situation. He then insisted that I took the train into service and I quickly deduced that he knew nothing about '63 stock or the rule book. He argued that time was money, customers would be unhappy, and that the service would be severely disrupted if I did 'not get on with it!' I could not believe my ears and told him in no uncertain terms that the 'customers' would also be upset if they were involved in a train crash when I made an attachment at Haywards Heath! I again refused to work the train and made a point that the unit was not already out on the main line, where customers would have to be de-trained anyway. It was right next to a maintenance depot where the fault could be repaired. I was then threatened with disciplinary action if I refused to work the train. I still refused and the situation became heated. The Control room got wind of what was occurring and I was handed another telephone. They, very clearly, told me to ignore the manager and hang up the phone on him, stating that they would deal with him later. Another train was commandeered for me and the dud was dragged into Lover's Walk by another 4 CIG. I never heard the outcome of what happened to the manager but he was quite high up in the scheme of things so the incident was probably quietly forgotten. I was not disciplined and I made a point of contacting the fitters to see if they had found a problem. There was indeed a serious fault in the brake chest on the leading driving trailer. I never heard another word about it and I was not even asked to fill out a report, which was unusual in itself!

It would seem that electrical faults were even rarer than brake faults and I only experienced two in my time on '63 stock. The first was when driving an evening commuter service from Victoria to Bognor Regis via Hove. When taking notch two, 'series', the front unit in the twelve car formation kept overloading. The two units on the rear where fine so they banged hard into the front one each time I pulled away and notched up the power handle. The overload reset button worked each time that I used it but it took a long time to get any speed out of the train. I had to put the unit into notch one 'shunt' and let the speed build up to about fifteen mph before attempting to notch up gradually into 'series' which didn't always work. The ride was pretty rough so I contacted the signalman and explained that I could keep going but was losing time hand over fist. He contacted the Control room and they requested that I should continue in service and do my best to get to Bognor where I eventually arrived thirty minutes late. When I reported the faulty unit to the fitters at Brighton it came as no surprise. They said that it had been in on the previous week and that a fault had been found on the 'series' circuit. They thought that they had rectified it but something in the unit must have been causing it to re-occur so they would have to look into it more seriously. The unit was detached from the train and then shunted into the sidings to await an empty stock move to Lover's Walk. I drove it a few days later and it behaved impeccably. The fitters must have delved a little deeper into the unit's wiring circuits.

The second, possible, electrical fault occurred when driving an empty twelve car formation from Lover's Walk depot to London Victoria. I then had to work it from Victoria to Littlehampton as an evening commuter service. The empty stock working to Victoria was booked to take a rather protracted two hours and it ran via Norwood Junction and Crystal Palace. It was then due to sit on the signal, which protected Balham Junction, for about ten minutes. This signal was situated next to the carriage washer road at Streatham Hill. All empty stock workings were booked to run D.O.O. by this time. This was not an ideal situation because trains were occasionally stopped on signals which were adjacent to platforms. Normally, drivers would 'signal crawl' along the platform until a 'proceed' aspect was displayed but occasionally, a signalman would ask the driver to pull up to the signal so that the track circuit in the rear could be cleared. It was then very difficult to get away from a platform without a guard to see the train out. It was made doubly hard if the platform was on the offside. Doors were very rarely locked on slam door stock so passengers could attempt to board the train as it pulled away. As a driver, there was no way of knowing if something had gone wrong when pulling away under these circumstances. This trip however, went very well until I reached the entrance of Leigham Court tunnel, which was just short of Streatham Hill station.

The line indicator flag flickered, showing that I had lost the juice momentarily. A blip in the traction current was not unusual and I continued through the tunnel with a little power applied. The signals showed that I did indeed have to stop at Balham Junction. I lost the juice again when approaching the signal so I stopped and put the brake into full service. This time, the current did not come back on. Victoria signal box called and informed me that the electrical control room were saying that my train was the cause of the current dropping out. I asked for a temporary block on the down line so that I could inspect the train on both sides in case something was hanging down and shorting out the conductor rail. This was refused because the service was approaching the rush hour peak so I checked one side of the train but could find nothing amiss. I returned to the front cab and the current was still off. I checked the offside of the train by walking carefully along the cess on the down line. Still nothing untoward could be seen so I contacted the signalman and asked if the E.C.R. was sure that it was my train. It had, after all, behaved perfectly well for the last hour and a half. The E.C.R. was still insistent that my train was the cause of the problem so I informed the signalman that I was about to carry out the 'paddling up' procedure. This would involve placing a wooden paddle between each collector shoe and the conductor rail. I would then remove the paddles from one unit at a time to see if the current could be restored. This process of elimination would hopefully point to the faulty unit, if indeed there was one.

The signalman called again and told me to sit tight because the E.C.R. were going to try to restore the up line traction current by diverting the power supply from the down carriage sidings. This worked, to my relief and the signal came off. With some trepidation, I pulled away gently and the train snaked through the crossovers on to the up Brighton fast line, eventually arriving at Victoria three quarters of an hour late. I was not convinced that the fault had been with my train, although I could not find out what had caused it. The train did not affect the supply once the current had been restored and the units worked as they should have for the run down to the coast. It had been a hot summer's day and I was glad to leave the units at Littlehampton. It had been hard to trust them, once the doubt had been put in my mind!

The last fault didn't really affect my duty too badly. I was working with a twelve car train on the 23.02 Brighton to Victoria service. This was my first working of the evening on the Brighton turn which was commonly known as the 'Night Gatwicks'. On arrival at East Croydon, I was informed that there was smoke coming from a bogie under the 4 VEP at the rear of the train. It turned out to be a hot axle box and luckily for me, there was a Selhurst crew waiting in the staff room on the platform. They were booked 'pass' back to depot and they kindly detached the unit and took it into Selhurst where the fitters could sort out the problem. I continued on to Victoria with the remaining eight coaches where I arrived just a few minutes late.

HUMAN ERROR!

Momentary lack of concentration could literally make a driver's toes curl up! I missed two station stops during my ten years of driving. In my defence, they were both 'out of the ordinary' stops. Luckily, I got away with both! The first station that I missed was at a small village called Glynde. I was working on an early turn which began with an empty stock move from Brighton to Haywards Heath. From there, I worked the four car unit down to Eastbourne, via Plumpton and Lewes. I had worked hundreds of services along this route but most originated from London. I therefore habitually thought that I would only call at Polegate after leaving Lewes because this was the norm on Victoria to Eastbourne services. The Brighton to Eastbourne services normally took in the more rural stops along the line.

I did not check my diagram and with my brain in 'Down London' mode, I hurtled through Glynde at line speed! The guard popped his head around the door and casually mentioned that we were booked to stop 'all stations' from Lewes. I shut off the power and coasted very slowly to the next stop at Berwick where the signalman may have suspected something if I had arrived three or four minutes early. I got away with it, almost! The station supervisor was waiting for me when I arrived at Eastbourne. A lady had phoned from Glynde to say that her train had 'raced' through the station! Luckily, a Brighton train had picked her up just a few minutes later and I had not been reported for the incident. The lady came into the staff office when she arrived at Eastbourne. There was a cup of tea waiting for her because the station supervisor had promised that the driver of the offending train would get her a cuppa and apologise in person. This I did and all was graciously accepted. I spent the rest of the turn expecting a traction inspector to pop out of the woodwork with a 'please explain' form and some points to put on my licence. It didn't happen and I did stop at Glynde on the only other occasion that I worked on this train.

A year later I was working on the Victoria to Three Bridges return run which was in the middle of the 'Night Gatwicks' turn. I had a smooth run from Victoria to East Croydon where the signalman called me on the cab radio. He asked me what speed I had been travelling at as I drove the train through Selhurst. I thought that this was a rather strange question but I replied "something in the region of sixty miles per hour." He laughed and informed me that I should have stopped to pick up staff at Selhurst. I looked at my diagram and, sure enough, the Selhurst stop was on there! He laughed again and then informed me that a Thameslink driver was going to report me for 'failing to call'. The Thameslink man must have eventually made his way to wherever he was going by another form of transport because there were no other trains booked to stop in the small hours. I was not reported and it would have been very unusual for one driver to tell tales on another. I did, again, spend the rest of the shift waiting for a 'please explain' form!

I had a lucky escape, on one afternoon, from what could have been a very embarrassing incident on platform six at Brighton. I was due to work a semi-fast service to Victoria, and having put my key on, I wound the roller blinds to the '34' headcode and popped to the toilet which was at the rear end of my driving trailer. I answered the call of nature with three minutes to go until departure. I then washed my hands and froze in horror because there was no handle on the inside of the toilet door! Although everybody did it, drivers were never supposed to leave the cab with a key 'on'. The cab door was also supposed to be locked, but wasn't. All that I had in my pocket was a carriage key and the penknife which I always carried at work. I spent the next two minutes, with sweat rolling down my forehead, removing screws from the handle back-plate with my knife. Once that was off, I used the carriage key to open the door. I threw all the screws and parts into the sink and locked the door from the outside. I ran back to the cab and sat down as the guard rang the bell for the off. From then on, I got into the habit of checking that a door handle was present when using the loo on '63 stock!

I did have one other door incident. It occurred on a very chilly morning and involved a rather silly oversight when detaching a unit at Haywards Heath. I was due to work the rear portion of a Victoria to Eastbourne train, the front portion heading for somewhere on the West Coastway. I had just had a break on the station and when the train rolled in the guard said that he had closed all the doors between the units. The train was late arriving and this helped to save a little time when carrying out the detachment. I split the units and blew the horn to inform the driver of the front unit that the detachment was complete. I put up the correct headcode, asked the guard for a brake test, and set off towards Wivelsfield when the signal came off. The train must have been running at about 60mph when there was a very loud bang as the front corridor connection vestibule door blew wide open! I had not noticed that the guard had not bolted it and there was a whoosh of freezing cold air pouring into the cab. I looked around the small wall on the right hand side of the driver's cubicle in sheer disbelief. The sleepers were rushing past under the front of the train and I could not reach the door to close it and secure one of the bolts. I did not want to stop the train out of course because this may have raised unwanted questions from the signalman so I decreased the speed and locked the door firmly shut on arrival at Wivelsfield. With hindsight, it was quite a funny incident and the look on my face must have been a picture as the door flew open. I should have double checked that all was as it should be before starting off and never again took it for granted that the front vestibule door was bolted after a detachment had been carried out. In any case, the driver usually prepared the doors so I didn't say anything to the guard on arrival at Eastbourne. I imagine he thought that he had done me a favour in helping out!

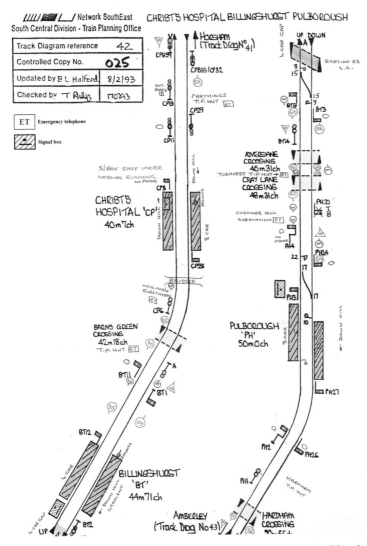

Route map section of the Mid-Sussex line. Semaphore signals predominate although all distant signals were of the colour light variety. Note the 4 car 'gap' on the up line at Billingshurst.
Author's collection

My next error came when driving a VEP + CIG eight car formation from London Bridge to Bognor Regis. It was a dark winter's evening and the train was very busy until I began to stop at stations on the Mid-Sussex line below Horsham. I will never know why, but the colour light distant signal did not register when approaching Pulborough on the downhill gradient. It was dark and the semaphore home signal for Pulborough appeared as I came out of one of the curves. The signal was only a very short distance from the beginning of the platform ramp. The train was still running at around 60mph and my braking mark was a long way behind me. I applied a full service application and my toes did indeed curl up as the train passed the platform ramp at somewhere in the region of 45mph. The distant signal would have registered if it had been 'on' because I would have had to cancel the AWS. Thus alerted, I would also have braked at my normal mark. My fate was in the hands of the E.P. brake which was an excellent piece of equipment on '63 stock. I let the brake off, so as to stop smoothly, right next to the eight car mark on the platform. It was a minor miracle that I had got away with it. I am sure that I would have flown right through the station if the train had been disc brake fitted! I did prefer to drive trains that were fitted with traditional brake blocks. Disc brakes, although managed by the train when on poor rail head conditions, did not clean the muck off the wheels which could cause a train to slide. I never overshot anywhere with either type of brake but an E.P. braked unit was always far superior on wet, dry or contaminated rails.

My last mistake was also avoidable and I'm glad that I didn't get caught for it. I was on my first day back at work after a holiday in Scotland and the 377s had replaced the 319s on the fast Brighton to Victoria services. There was a short section of line, between Balcombe Tunnel Junction and Three Bridges, which had been cleared for 100mph running. I was driving a nine car formation of 377s at 80mph and when I exited Balcombe Tunnel I decided to put the units to the test. I was driving at 100mph in no time at all! I had a personal needs break when I returned to Brighton and I happened to mention to a fellow driver that I was very impressed by the acceleration of the 377s when already running at high speed. He reminded me that 319s were still the only units cleared for 100mph running on the Brighton line! A notice had come out, while I was on holiday, stating that the 377s were only cleared for a maximum speed of 90mph. I had made a mistake in not reading the notices which were issued while I was away from the job. I looked them up and my fellow driver had been right!

I must add that all train drivers are, without exception, very responsible people and are very diligent when carrying out their duties. Drivers, just like other human beings, are prone to the occasional minor error. This and a little complacency were the main contributors to the above incidents and I'm pleased to say that these were my only sins over the ten year period.

ANTISOCIAL BEHAVIOUR

It is unfortunate that a section covering this topic is required but dealing with vandalism and mindless behaviour has become part of a train driver's job. As can be seen from my own experiences, the most prolific offenders were teenage boys and young men. Smaller crimes, such as daubing trains in the sidings with graffiti or etching 'tags' into the train windows with glass cutters, were irritating and mindless but were not dangerous to anybody but the actual offenders who were committing the crime. Serious thoughtlessness, such as laying ballast on the rails, could have had more dangerous consequences. This happened to me one afternoon when working on a Portsmouth Harbour to Brighton stopping service. I noticed eight or nine lumps of ballast on one running rail when approaching Emsworth on the return journey. Two teenagers were running away from the scene as I braked hard and hit the ballast at about 30mph. The 4 CIG's driving trailer bumped over the rocks but somehow managed to stay on the track. I went back to inspect the line and there were dusty smudges on the running rail where the ballast had been obliterated. The lads were long gone but I phoned the signalman and asked him to warn other drivers that vandals were in the vicinity. The consequences of this incident can only be imagined if there had been a derailment. The section of line ran along a steep sided high embankment.

I had two more close shaves on the West Coastway. The first was when I was working a stopping service between Littlehampton and Brighton. Somebody threw half of a house brick at the front of the train as I approached Angmering. It flew across the front of my cab window and hit the vestibule door on the corridor connection. There was a rather large dent in the door when I inspected the train.

The second incident was actually quite chilling. This happened when working an afternoon Brighton to Portsmouth Harbour stopping service. The stoppers were often booked to run 'fast' through Hilsea station as it was generally only used by workers from the industrial estate during peak periods. My train was not booked to stop and I was running at somewhere near the line speed of 85mph. There was a footbridge a short distance beyond Hilsea and there was a young man standing on it, waving his hand. As a driver, you could never help being suspicious when confronted by a youth in this kind of situation. I gingerly waved back, only to see the young man raise his other hand which was holding a whole house brick. He very casually let go of it! I ducked and there was an almighty bang somewhere on the front of the unit. My natural reaction was to blow the horn, more out of anger than anything else! There was no point in trying to stop the train, and after informing the signalman of what had happened, I pulled into Fratton station to inspect the unit. The air horn, which was situated just above my cab window, looked as if it had exploded. It was split and had peeled back in strips like a banana skin. Incredibly, it still made a loud noise when operated! I will never forget the calm look on the young man's face as he let go of the brick. It was the most callous act that I came across in my ten years of driving and it could well have killed me and endangered the train.

Soon after this incident, I ran across a line of detonators which had been placed on the running rail at Angmering level crossing. They had been laid on the track by youths who had no thought of the injuries that may have been caused to members of the public who were waiting to cross the line. Stealing detonators from the rear cabs of slam door units was a bit of a lark with youngsters for a short period. Unfortunately, '63 stock cabs were locked with a carriage key and the locks were no obstacle to determined youths.

I had two unfortunate incidents when driving along the East Coastway. The first was when I was working on an evening stopping service from Portsmouth Harbour to Seaford via Brighton. All 'seemed' to go well along the West Coastway and I changed ends in platform three at Brighton before heading off along the East Coastway towards Lewes. The guard called me on the loudaphone and informed me that there was smoke coming from the roof of the front driving trailer as we pulled out of Falmer station. I am not sure why he didn't tell me before we had pulled away. I told the guard to evacuate the coach and lock it out of service immediately. Following this, I looked back out of the cab window but could see nothing. The line between Falmer and Lewes runs on a mixture of high embankments and deep cuttings. I decided to keep going because there was no access for the emergency services. I called ahead to the signalman and requested that the fire brigade should meet us on arrival at Lewes. There was indeed a lot of smoke coming from the rear end of the coach by the time I stopped the train in the platform. I applied the handbrake and ran to the brake van to cut the unit out. The guard de-trained the passengers and the fire brigade arrived moments later. Leaving the train in capable hands, I decided to phone the fitters at Brighton to see if they would have a clue as to what may have started the fire. The reply came back that there was a good chance of it being caused by somebody smoking in the toilet. The fitter that I spoke to told me that he would shortly be on his way to Lewes in the van, adding that he didn't want the CIG torn to pieces by the firemen. It was too late for that because, by this time, the fire was belching black smoke into the night sky. Luckily it was extinguished very quickly, although the toilet ceiling had been torn down in the process. The chief fireman was convinced that somebody had put a lit cigarette through a ventilator grille in the ceiling. The fitter arrived soon after and was not pleased when he inspected the damage to the unit! The lighting conduit had caught alight and a lot of it had burned away and melted. I cut the unit back in and tripped out all of the lighting circuits after letting the damage cool down for a while. The passengers were supplied with taxis and I returned the unit to Brighton where I ran it into Lover's Walk shed.

Smoking was banned on trains by then and smokers would occasionally 'lose' a cigarette, wherever they could, if they thought that the guard was in the near vicinity. This sort of thing happened now and then and I thought that would be an end to the matter as I drove home wearily along the coast road. I could not have been more mistaken! I was on the same train on the following day and, having put the fire of the previous evening behind me, I was rather surprised at what I saw when I stopped at Southwick station on the West Coastway. There were five young lads standing in a line, directly opposite my cab, on the down platform. They were loudly chanting the same sentence over and over again. "Burn, burn, the roof's on fire! Burn, burn, the roof's on fire!" This was obviously for my benefit and it was rather creepy to say the least. The guard rang the bell and I opened up the power handle very quickly. I had never seen these lads before but I guessed that they had had something to do with the previous evening's mischief. I can only assume that they found entertainment in risking the safety of the passengers and crew on board the train.

The second incident happened on the East Coastway when I was working an evening stopping service from Hastings to Brighton. I had just pulled away from Cooden Beach when I noticed a young lad driving a Ford XR2 along the lane which runs alongside the railway line. The lane meets the line a little further on at Pevensey Sluice level crossing. The XR2 stayed parallel with my train for a short time but I did not really think much of it. The car then suddenly shot off at an amazing rate of knots as I gradually gained speed. A thought flashed across my mind that the driver was trying to outrun me to the level crossing. As a driver, I had been taught not to allow myself to be windy about this sort of thing so I kept the power handle wide open. I could see the level crossing warning lights flashing ahead of me and the car followed the road as it looped around to face the track at ninety degrees. It stopped at the crossing and by this time the train was travelling at about 60mph. The lad floored the accelerator again and zigzagged the automatic half barrier crossing right in front of the train. I instinctively blew the horn and the train missed the car by three or four coach lengths. The car disappeared around a bend in moments and I was left in disbelief at the stupidity of the driver. It was dark and there was no way that he could have reasonably judged the distance and speed of my approaching train. Part of the job was to carry on with what you were doing and not be too upset with irresponsible behaviour that was sometimes displayed by younger, less experienced individuals. A driver's living depended upon working and there was a saying that near misses didn't *actually* happen so it was best to put them to the back of your mind and get on with the job. This certainly worked for most people but drivers never forgot incidents that could have risked their and other people's lives.

UNUSUAL OCCURRENCES

I came very close to running down members of the permanent way staff on two occasions. These occurrences can only be put down to a lack of concentration on the part of the people who were involved. The first incident happened on approach to Portsmouth and Southsea, just after I had left Fratton with a stopping service from Brighton. I was passing a unit on the up line while braking for the 15mph speed restriction on approach to the high level down platform. The tail end of the unit passed me and a man stepped into the track directly behind it. He then proceeded to step into the track in front of my train, without first checking to see if the down line was clear. I blew the horn and the man jumped backwards into the up line before I managed to make an emergency brake application. It all happened very quickly and I missed him by about half a coach length!

The second incident happened on the up fast line, when approaching Balham. I was driving a loaded twelve car train and had just slowed for the 60mph speed restriction before the station. There is a left hand curve on approach and as I rounded it I saw that there was a 'lookout' standing on the platform ramp. I blew the horn but the man didn't react by raising one arm to acknowledge that he had seen me. He did not blow his warning horn either so I blew the train horn harder and longer but the man still didn't react. I wrongly assumed that the permanent way staff, who he was supposed to be looking out for, were probably some distance off and were on another line. Six men dived down the steep embankment to the left as I came out of the curve. There was no time for them to jump up on to the island platform because I was probably two or three coach lengths from the nearest man, who happened to be working between the running rails. I had instinctively braked but knew that it would not have made much difference had the men on the track been slower off the mark. I did not report the incident because it would not have changed anything but I am sure that the lookout would probably have had a bit of a telling off from his co-workers! Again, the incident happened very quickly and the usual curling of the toes took place for a few seconds before carrying on with the journey to Victoria.

The most unusual close shave that I had came when driving a 4 CIG unit on the outward journey of a Brighton to West Worthing return service. I had just crossed the Adur river bridge and had shut the power off at 65mph. The train would coast for a while before braking for the next stop at Lancing. This stretch of line passes close to Shoreham airport which is on the right hand side of the track. The airport is fairly small and generally only sees the use of light aircraft. I thought I saw something white, out of the corner of my eye, through the side window as I passed the airport. It was only a fleeting glimpse and I was not sure what it was that I had seen. A second later, it revealed itself to be a light aircraft and it flew directly across the path of my train! It was roughly four coach lengths in front of me and the landing wheels were about six feet above the height of the track. I did not have time to apply the brakes as it all happened so quickly. I did however call Lancing signal box to report the incident. I was a little shaken for a couple of seconds before the instinct to carry on kicked in. The signalman asked me if I would like to be 'taken off' and relieved by another driver but I declined the offer and finished the round trip back to Brighton. I paid a visit to the head traction inspector who had already been informed of what had happened. He promptly telephoned the British Transport Police office after hearing my account of the story. This had apparently happened before but my close shave had been the closest one yet. I did not find out if any action was taken against the pilot of the plane but I did find out why the incident had happened. When landing, pilots were supposed to pass a certain mark on the runway before touching down. Landing past the mark kept the aircraft at a safe approach angle above the railway line. It was discovered that pilots were landing at the beginning of the runway so that they could taxi off at an earlier exit, thus saving themselves a little time. It is interesting to think that, so far, there has never been an accident which involved an aircraft crashing into a train. I tried not to think about it when I next drove past Gatwick Airport!

I used the emergency brake in anger on only one occasion when approaching a signal. I had just left Ford on a Victoria to Bognor Regis service and was running at the line speed of 65mph. It was dark and the view ahead was clear when signal BH101 suddenly turned from green to red. This signal protected the level crossing at Yapton. I threw the brakes into emergency and the train lurched to a grinding halt at about twenty feet short of the signal. I uncurled my toes; BH101 had reverted to green as the train stopped. I stayed put and called the signalman at Barnham to ask if he knew what had happened. He stated that he had replaced the signal to danger in order to carry out a shunt move in the station, adding that he did not realise that I was so close to BH101. I was not pleased. Signalmen were always supposed to give warning before placing a signal back to danger in front of a moving train. I received an apology after explaining that it had crossed my mind that something may have been amiss on the level crossing ahead. I then told the signalman that he could have arranged for Arundel box to give me a cautionary aspect on the signal preceding BH101. The guard was not too pleased either because he had had some complaints about the exceedingly rough stop! I went to the signal box on arrival at Barnham and, after apologising again, the signalman asked me to fill out a report form when I arrived at Bognor Regis. Genuine mistakes did happen now and then. I accepted the apology and, unsurprisingly, never heard another word about the matter.

Signalmen and drivers were, in general, like chalk and cheese. Drivers would complain if they were held needlessly on signals and likewise, signalmen would complain if they thought drivers were driving too slowly. An unusual occurrence happened when driving an eight car train, formed with 1963 stock, between Eastbourne and Haywards Heath. It was during the autumn 'leaf fall' season and it was just beginning to get dark. Due to the large number of trees on the line side, the line between Lewes and Keymer Junction was notorious for being slippery at this time of year. I had recently driven through Plumpton station at speed, only to see that the distant signal was 'on' for the signal which protected Spatham Lane level crossing. I began to brake, very gently at first, applying only 5 pounds per square inch to the brake cylinders which was enough to clean the muck from the wheels. I very carefully slowed the train down and crawled up to T644 signal which was still at danger, protecting the level crossing. The signal turned to green as the train stopped. I opened the power handle to notch one, in the hope that I could get the train moving on the gentle uphill gradient. I also opened the cab window so that I could listen for wheel spin as I pulled away. The spin was instantaneous so I shut off the power and tried again, and again, and again. It took quite some time for the train to reach 6 or 7mph. The cab radio beeped and Three Bridges signal box called to tell me that they were doing an 'adhesion survey'. I informed the box that I didn't really have any adhesion and was having great difficulty in getting the train up to any speed. The signalman had literally stopped the train to see if the track in the area was contaminated with leaf fall sludge. I was asked if I had had any trouble stopping the train and I replied that it was lucky that I hadn't because there had been a red light and level crossing ahead of me! I explained that I could have stopped the train at Plumpton to test the adhesion in the area. I patiently went through the adhesion survey questions with the radio handset tucked under my chin and my head out of the window because I still needed to listen out for wheel spin. In the end, it took me fifteen minutes of hand notching to reach Keymer Junction where the line connects with the Brighton line to London. This distance would have been covered in about two minutes under normal running conditions. Signalmen, although they held up trains for no apparent reason on occasion, also did their jobs very diligently. This was only the second occasion when I thought that what had happened was totally unnecessary.

A strange thing happened along this stretch of line about a year prior to the adhesion incident. On the approach to Plumpton, there is a foot crossing which came out between high hedges on each side of the track. I was working on a twelve car commuter train to London when I hit something very hard on this crossing. I was used to hitting birds and was well aware that a wood pigeon could make quite a loud bang on the fibre glass front end of 1963 units. The bang was far louder than when hitting a pigeon and it seemed more to come from the lower half of the train, as if something had hit the buffers or bogie. Not knowing what I would find, I stopped to inspect the front of the unit. Had somebody stepped out from between the hedges as I went over the crossing at about 60mph? Incredibly, there was nothing to be seen but, to be on the safe side, I reported the incident to the signalman. He told me that he would send the next few trains, in both directions, through the section at caution, asking the drivers to keep an eye out for anything unusual. I was sure that the train had hit some kind of large object, person or animal but nothing amiss ever came of the incident. I still cannot imagine what could have caused such a loud bang on the front of the unit without leaving a trace of evidence.

Engineering works, either at night time or on Sundays, would quite often affect how a driver's duties were altered. At worst, a driver may have had to catch a bus to the far side of the works to continue with a duty. It was never good to have to mix with passengers under such circumstances. Understandably, they were not generally happy at the disruption which was being caused to their journey. More interesting situations did sometimes occur during engineering works. Occasionally, a driver would be called upon to act as a 'pilot' if diversionary routes were put into place. This involved riding in the cab and instructing a driver who was unfamiliar with the route. The pilot driver would relate the locations of junctions, signals, speed restrictions, braking marks and stopping marks. According to the rule book, the pilot driver was not allowed to drive, only to instruct. In some cases the pilot would not, in any case, be familiar with the type of traction which was being driven. Due to engineering works, the direct line between Brighton and Hove was shut on a particular Saturday. West Coastway services, in both directions, were diverted via Preston Park and the Cliftonville Spur. I can well remember relating the details of the route to some drivers whilst travelling in the second man's seat of class 158 units which were unfamiliar to me. Although it was short, the diversion was unfamiliar to the 'South West Trains' drivers so a lot of concentration was used on both sides.

I once drove along a very interesting diversionary route, with a pilot driver, on a summer Saturday. The down Brighton lines were shut between Battersea Park and Clapham Junction so main line trains from Victoria were diverted via Brixton and Herne Hill, eventually rejoining the main line at Streatham Common. I was due to work a twelve coach '63 stock train from Victoria to Brighton and came across my pilot driver when entering the cab. I did not recognise him but he introduced himself and said that he was there to guide me through the diversionary route. He confidently informed me that he was a bottom link Vic man and had only passed out for driving in the previous month! The guard rang the bell and I set off, rather dubiously, through the crossovers and on to the down slow line. A junction signal led us through the platforms at Battersea Park and the train snaked on to the Atlantic line. All was well and my young pilot seemed very confident with his route knowledge. He was not familiar with 1963 stock because the lower links at Victoria only worked suburban services with classes 319, 455 and

456. The experience was certainly strange and I felt like a blind man who was out with his guide dog for the first time. Luckily, the speed restrictions were fairly slow and I had plenty of time to react to my instructions. We came alongside the South Eastern section 'Chatham lines' at Wandsworth Road Junction/station. We then pottered through Voltaire Road Junction and Clapham High Street station before crossing on to the Chatham lines at Shepherds Lane Junction. The route followed a continuous succession of junctions for its entire length. We next negotiated Canterbury Road Junction (sometimes known as Brixton Junction) where the Catford Loop diverges away to the left. We then coasted through the platform at Brixton and I applied a little power to take us to Herne Hill North Junction where the 'Holborn lines' come in from the left. We then ran through the platforms at Herne Hill. The Beckenham Junction lines pull away to the left at Herne Hill South Junction but we remained on the 'down Holborn' line and ran along to Tulse Hill North Junction where the 'Portsmouth lines' from London Bridge via North Dulwich come in from the left. We moved on to the 'down Portsmouth' line and coasted through Tulse Hill station. Tulse Hill South Junction was encountered next. From there, the lines to the left swing away to Crystal Palace and the lines to the right veer away to Streatham Hill and Balham. We arrived at Streatham after passing through Leigham and Streatham tunnels respectively. From there, we took the junction signal on to the Streatham Spur and crept away from the Portsmouth lines towards Streatham Common station. At last I was on home territory and I opened up the power and ran down the slow Brighton line to East Croydon. I thanked my pilot for his guidance when we arrived and he made his way back to Victoria for another journey. I have included, in my description, every junction and station which was encountered along the route. Added to these, there were many signals and speed restrictions to look out for, all of which, I was totally unfamiliar with at the time. It was to the young driver's credit that all went well and a lot of concentration was required from both of us on the twenty-five minute journey. The pilot, being new to the job, was also very enthusiastic and wanted to know all of the 'ins and outs' of what it was like be a driver at Brighton. I don't recall him ever pausing for breath along the entire route! Only the top link at Victoria went further south than the suburban area network so he would have had to wait for a very long time before getting a run down to the coast. I do not think that I would have enjoyed suburban work. Most of the turns were 'driver only operated' and nearly all of the workings were on stopping services so it must have made a pleasant change for these men to work on empty coaching stock!

It was rare to be put 'wrong road' as it was called, but things were always quite unusual when driving under the instruction of a pilotman. Single line working by pilotman did at least keep the trains running and it helped to

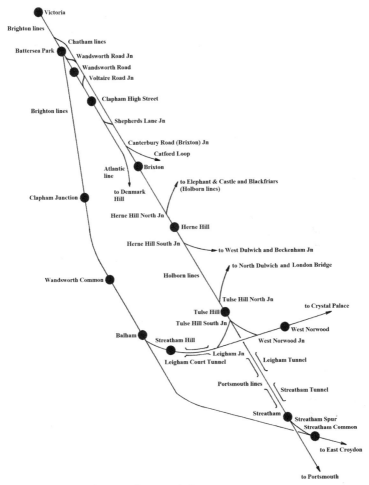

The Victoria to Streatham Common diversion. *Author*

avoid the dreaded replacement bus services. Trains were normally driven at slower speeds when under these conditions but higher speeds were involved if single line working was in place on the southern half of the Brighton line. Bi-directional signalling was in place between Preston Park and Balcombe Tunnel Junction and a pilotman was supplied if one of the two lines was blocked for engineering works. The down line, between Preston Park and Hassocks, was blocked on one particular Sunday and I had a duty which involved working three shuttles between Brighton and Hassocks. The pilotman was not required on the 'up' trip but I was briefed by him on arrival at Hassocks. He reminded me of the speed restrictions and informed me that we would be travelling back to Brighton on the 'up' line. It was always very odd and seemed to go against the grain when driving on the opposite line to which you had become accustomed. Clayton tunnel is on this stretch of line and there were no temporary speed restrictions in place on this particular day. The line speed when driving in the 'up' direction, on the 'up' line, was 90mph whereas the speed when driving 'down' the 'up' line was set at 75mph. My hand hovered over the brake handle because it was very strange to be travelling at speed, on what felt like the wrong track, through a tunnel which was well over a mile long!

The tunnel had a notorious reputation because there had been several accidents inside its 1 mile and 499 yard length. In the early days, trains were merely 'timed' at intervals through the tunnel and in 1861 three successive trains were involved in a terrible accident which resulted in the deaths of 22 people and left 177 injured. The beginnings of modern signalling practices spawned from the lessons learned from this accident. To add to the reputation, four soldiers had been killed by a train when hiding in the tunnel on a practice exercise in 1973.

Balcombe tunnel seemed to have a more benevolent nature. It was commonly known as the Balcombe carriage washer because, even in the driest weather, the 'up' line through the tunnel was particularly wet. This came in very handy for washing the windscreen on 1963 stock because these units were not fitted with windscreen washers like the more modern units. I did have one interesting occurrence which involved this tunnel. It was early on a Saturday evening and I was driving a semi-fast service from Victoria to Brighton. I could not be sure, but I thought that I had heard a dull thud when entering the tunnel at the line speed of 80mph. The guard knocked on the cab door by the time we reached Balcombe station and he asked me if I could get Three Bridges signal box to arrange for an ambulance to meet us at Haywards Heath. He then disappeared, saying that all would be revealed on arrival. I called the signalman and did as the guard had requested. On arrival at 'The Heath', the guard and some other men helped a shirtless man out of the compartment which was directly behind my cab. The man was extremely drunk and his mates, as the men had turned out to be, were helping him to stand up straight and telling him to stay still. I had indeed heard a thud when entering Balcombe tunnel. The men had been soaked to the skin, by a heavy shower, while at a football match in London and the drunken man had been drying his football shirt by holding it at arm's length out of the window. His arm had hit the tunnel portal and, as I later found out from the station supervisor, had been broken in seven places! There was also a large open gash which, incredibly, was not bleeding. The man was so drunk that he didn't really seem to know what had happened but he must have been extremely sore once he had sobered up. Luckily, there was one small bit of good news for him. He had let go of his shirt when his arm hit the tunnel portal but it had caught on the butterfly at the rear of the leading driving trailer. The shirt had miraculously stayed in place until removed by the guard at Haywards Heath!

Occasionally, the smallest incident or oversight would affect the way in which a train would be worked. I drove a few units which had clear glass sun visors that made signal sighting very tricky in bright conditions. The visors were normally fitted with brown tinted glass which was a vast improvement when heading towards the sun. On one occasion, a small fitting came loose and made an afternoon journey from Brighton to Victoria very uncomfortable. I had just pulled away from Brighton and had begun to run the train through the crossovers which led on to the main line. As the train straightened out, the theatre style seat decided that it could not hold my weight any longer! It collapsed and I dropped down on to the floor. I somehow kept hold of the power handle and, in a very dazed fashion, I managed to stand up and regain my composure. The look of surprise on my face must have been worth its weight in gold! The rest of the journey, which was a semi-fast working via Redhill, was hard going. I would sometimes stand up for a change of position but not for the entire length of the Brighton line and my legs were like jelly by the time I pulled into Victoria. I found the brake handle on '63 stock much easier to adjust with my elbow resting comfortably on the narrow cab side windowsill. The standing position did not cater for this so I stopped at most stations in a stooped, contorted position, with my elbow still on the sill which must have looked a little strange to anybody who saw me. I found the Victoria station fitter and he managed to do a botched repair job on the seat. I was due to return to Brighton and then work the units back to London again so the repair was very necessary!

A small, but significant, event happened in 2001 when I was working along the Coastway between Eastbourne and Hastings. I opened the cab side window as the train exited Bopeep tunnel. Two school boys came up to the cab, with a look of excitement on their faces, as I stopped the train in the platform at St Leonards. I said "Hello" and the boys informed me that Concorde had just crashed into the Empire State building in America! I laughed, amazed at the imagination required to conjure up such a story. Kids! The guard rang the bell and I pulled away into Hastings tunnel. I pondered on what the odds would be of such an iconic aircraft hitting an equally iconic building; I guessed that they would be pretty low. I changed ends at Hastings and worked my last train of the day back to Brighton. I didn't see anybody to speak to between Hastings and home and while changing out of my uniform, I put the television on to listen to the news headlines. I often did this just to relax after a shift. It was the 11th of September and I listened in disbelief as I learned that two aircraft had been deliberately crashed into the World Trade Centre's twin towers in New York. The school boys had not quite got the facts right but the real incident far outweighed the odds that I was thinking about in Hastings tunnel. As for many people, it was one of those days where I would always remember where I was when I first heard the story. Even if the first version of it was, to say the least, very unlikely!

There became a problem with storage space as more and more 377 units were delivered to Brighton. The 'Wall' sidings, on the western side of Brighton station, were re-opened to house slam door units and Newhaven Marine platform and siding were regularly utilised for the overnight berthing of twelve car trains. Drivers on 'spare' duties would be called upon to move the outcast units to Newhaven for the night. The siding was later used to store '63 stock before it was hauled away to the scrap yards. It was good to see Newhaven Marine back in use for a short time, but not for such a lamentable task! I was on the 6.00am spare duty one morning and had been given instructions to get myself over to Newhaven with a guard. We were to prepare a twelve car CIG formation because the train was needed for a commuter service between Brighton and London. The train was stone cold and the brakes were 'flat' when we arrived at Newhaven. It took a little while to pump it up and during this time we unlocked the doors along each side of the units. It was unusual for anything to be locked but vandalism was a consideration and there were no staff in the area to keep an eye on things. We carried out a brake test and waited for the signal arm to be raised at the end of the platform. The signal came off and I opened up the power handle gently. I had it in mind that the Newhaven substation was a bit of a weakling. I refer back to the above mentioned sectional appendix local instruction which stated: if more than one unit was to be used on the Seaford branch, the train was to be driven in no more than 'series'. I crept out of the platform at 15mph and made sure that the tail end of the train was well clear of the points before applying more power. I got the units into series for a short while and then coasted until I could see the signal which protected the level crossing at Newhaven Town. The signal came off and I began to apply a little more power. There was a four car gap just beyond the level crossing and I was eager to build up momentum so as to get the train across as quickly as possible. I worked the power handle up to notch three and was amazed to see that three conductor rail insulators were glowing red hot, just beyond the crossing. The insulators were known as 'pots' because they were made of very robust china. They were probably old ones which may have been cracked and so were leaking electricity to 'earth'. The weather was damp and this wouldn't have helped. The line normally had single units running along it and the pots were probably not used to carrying the amount of amps that a twelve car train could pull from the conductor rail when accelerating. I shut off the power and the units coasted, slowly, over the gap. The rear of the train cleared the crossing and, as far as I could tell, I managed to get the speed up to a reasonable level without blowing anything. The 10mph speed restriction at Lewes seemed to take a lifetime and once through it, I opened up the power handle to begin the climb up Falmer bank. Again, I noticed that a couple of pots were glowing so I shut off the power and re-applied a lesser amount. There was no room for coasting on Falmer bank. It is steep and curvy so I had to keep the pressure up on the conductor rail. I imagine that I would have heard something if any pots had actually blown because they were reputed to go quite well if old, damaged and wet! I had never seen this phenomenon before and I had wondered if 'glowing pots' were just a sort of railway urban legend. The rest of the journey went smoothly and it turned out to be the last time that I was to move '63 stock out of Newhaven Marine. The 377s had replaced most of the slam door rolling stock by this time and, as time passed, it was becoming rarer to get some time in on these old but very dependable units.

4 CIG 1854 (originally built as unit 7388) in Newhaven Marine siding. 13th April 2005. *Author*

Keeping the memories alive

The 1963 stock carried various liveries during my ten years of service. All Network SouthCentral units were wearing the red, white, blue and grey of Network Southeast when I began to drive but they were put into the yellow, white and blue of Connex South Central when this company took over the network. Some Connex units were nicknamed 'ghosts' by the train crews because they remained in a rather dull white undercoat for quite some time. Connex lost their franchise to Southern and, although many units were scrapped in Connex colours, some 4 CIGs were painted into their final livery of two-tone green, white and pale grey. The Southern livery was only applied to one 4 VEP unit, number 3514. Two 3 CIG units were specially repainted into commemorative liveries for use on the Lymington branch. Unit 1497 was painted in B.R. blue and grey while unit 1498 was painted in British Railways green livery. These units were, sadly, the last 1963 units to run in service.

Various units and coaches have been saved from the cutter's torch but it is debateable as to whether 1963 units will ever run on the main line again. The huge expense of having a unit certified for main line running can be overwhelming and enthusiasm, although it is there, may not be enough to raise the kind of funds that would be needed to lay a conductor rail on a preserved railway. It seems that memories of the units, more than anything else, are what will stay with me for the foreseeable future.

'Slammers' as they seem to have become affectionately known by their fan base, were never referred to as such by train crews. Phase one CIGs through to 1970s VEPs were known collectively as '63 stock and CEPs/BEPs were known as Kent Coasters or '57 stock. Southern electrics were often referred to by staff as 'Juicers' and some of the older motormen referred to them as 'Sparks' or 'Trams'.

Slam door stock did have some disadvantages. Occasionally, a new guard would quickly ring 'two' on the starting bell but the driver would only receive 'one' bell in the cab. One bell of course meant 'stop' so the driver would explain that it was best to operate the bell with a slight pause between rings. A door 'on the catch' at the rear of the train could be a nuisance and, occasionally, a draught from under the dashboard required a coat over the knees in winter. These were only small niggles and were easily overcome.

The failure rate of modern rolling stock is higher than that of these simple and more robust machines. One has only to listen to the travel bulletins on the radio to hear of frequent train failures which are no doubt caused by the complicated systems and computers that seem to be an everyday necessity in the modern world.

I have some particularly fond memories of working with 1963 stock. The sounds in Lover's Walk train depot were a pungent mix of throbbing compressors, whirring motor generators and squeals of flanges on sharp curves. The class 377 units have a driving cab which is not dissimilar to sitting in a plastic lined, portable toilet. The environment is clinically sterile and has no atmosphere or sense of history. The soft green of a '63 stock cab and the comfortable driving position of the theatre style seat had such a ring of 'Southern Electric' about it. The aroma of grease on the handbrakes and brake dust in a shirt collar all added to the relaxed atmosphere. It was amazing to look back out of the cab window when leaving London Victoria on a warm summer's evening. The rear of a twelve car train, 795 feet away, would snake through the crossovers while heat shimmered from the banks of resistances as power was applied for the climb up to Grosvenor Bridge and the crossing of the Thames. The 'Night Gatwicks' turn had an almost unreal quality and the self adjusting brake blocks would jingle when you drove with the window open to keep you fully alert. You would drive on empty lines, nearly all signals would be green and there were very few passengers; all of which was a rarity on the Southern! Brighton station could be very calm and atmospheric, especially on a dark and frosty morning. The 21.00 spare men would pump up the units, which had been left in the station overnight, in readiness for the early turn drivers who would work the first trains of the day. A good man would also make sure that the heaters were keeping the cabs nice and toasty!

During my time as a driver, the constant need for change saw the age old job title of traction inspector revamped to 'driver standards manager' and the train crew supervisors became 'production managers'. This latter title could describe virtually any managerial job in the land and does not even imply that these important members of staff work on the railway. Lover's Walk depot has been redesigned to accommodate class 377s and things have certainly moved on for the drivers since I was at Brighton. They no longer work on 319 units but now drive class 442s on the Gatwick Express services and class 313s on many of the Coastway duties. The 313s had a controversial beginning with Southern because they are very basic and are not fitted with toilets. This harks back to the pre-war days of the 2NOL units, NOL being the Southern Railway's unit code for 'No lavatory'. Passengers and commuters will never again be able to enjoy the luxury of Mark I coaches with sprung seat cushions and comfortable head rests. The jovial atmosphere of the buffet coach is also a thing of the past but the memories should be kept alive. One very necessary change took place in 2013. That hard to spot semaphore home signal at Newhaven Harbour was finally removed and was replaced by a very brightly illuminated LED colour light signal. Hard to spot it may have been, but to my knowledge, that semaphore signal had never been passed at danger without a signalman's permission. A testament to the fact that all drivers knew exactly where it was by instinct, even if it was not visible!

I was pleased to find out that I was the third train driver in my family whilst in the process of writing this book. Although a distant relative, the 1881 census shows that a man, on my grandfather's side of the family, was an engine driver somewhere in East Suffolk. The 1911 census shows that my great, great uncle, who was also on my grandfather's side, was a driver by the age of thirty on the Liverpool Overhead Railway. The line, commonly known as the 'docker's umbrella' because the Liverpool dockers used it for sheltering under in poor weather, was operated with electric trains. It would have been magnificent if these two gentlemen had written accounts of their experiences and also to see if they were as proud as I am to have been a train driver.

4 CEP 7105 at the East Kent Railway on 30th March 2013. The unit is in the care of the EPB Preservation Group and at the time of writing is undergoing restoration to its original unrefurbished state. *Author*

Appendix

TRAIN PREPARATION AND BRAKE TESTS ON 1963 STOCK

This section reflects the official guidelines which were set out for 1963 stock train preparation and brake testing. I have included this information so as to provide a fully rounded picture of a driver's responsibilities when working with this particular type of rolling stock.

PREPARING A TRAIN FOR SERVICE

- Check that no red flags or 'Not to be moved boards' are displayed. The buffers should be retracted and the buckeye coupling should be raised. The dual air cocks should be closed with the pipes stowed in their recesses.
- In the leading cab: Check that the handbrake/parking brake is on. Insert the E.P. key and turn the master switch to 'on' which will cause the A.W.S. warning horn to sound. The A.W.S. button must be depressed and released to cancel the warning horn.
- Place the brake selector switch to E.P and charge the main reservoir pipe by placing the brake handle to the emergency position. Place the brake handle in the release position once the main reservoir is charged to between 90 and 100lb/psi, this charges the brake pipe to a minimum of 65lb/psi and the brakes release. Place the brake handle to 10 to 20lb/psi.
- Turn the headlight and headcode illumination on, put up the correct headcode and set up the cab secure radio.
- Check that the following equipment is present in the cab: fire extinguisher, track circuit operating clips, detonators and flags, short circuiting bar, hook switch pole, shoe fuse spanner, 2x paddles and wheel scotches if on an electric parking brake unit.
- Check that all miniature circuit breakers are set, that the horn works and that the front vestibule door is bolted. Check that the red A.W.S. isolating handle is in the correct position, with the seal intact. Check that the T.P.W.S. is not isolated.
- Leave the cab and check that the headlight is on.
- Proceed along the side of the train checking the shoe gear and ribbon fuses, that equipment covers are closed, that cables and pipes between vehicles are connected and are not hanging down. Make sure all doors are properly closed.
- Climb into the brake van, check that the unit is cut in and turn the train lights on. Check that miniature circuit breakers are set and that fuses are in place with spares available. Check safety equipment is present, i.e. track circuit operating clips, ladder, fire

extinguisher, crowbar and emergency screw coupling. The emergency equipment cupboard should be locked.

- Carry out the above along the entire length of the train. Check in intermediate cabs that: no E.P. keys or handbrakes are 'on', brake handles are in the release position and black blanks are displayed in the headcode boxes. Check both sides of the train if possible, including connections between units, i.e. pipes, dual air cocks, jumpers and couplings. Check coupling, pipes and jumper on the rear end of the train, making sure that the headlight is switched 'off'.
- In the rear cab: In addition to the above, check that the headcode illumination is 'on' and red roller blinds are displayed.
- Walk through the interior of the train, checking that fire extinguishers are present and that all doors, which are required to be locked, are locked.
- Return to the leading driving cab, carry out brake tests and take the handbrake/parking brake off.

DRIVER'S PERSONAL BRAKE TEST

E.P. brake test:

- Place the brake handle to full service. The brake cylinder gauge should climb to approximately 50lb/psi. Return the brake handle to approx. 20lb/psi.

Westinghouse auto brake test:

- Place the brake selector switch to auto with the brake cylinder pressure at approximately 20lb/psi. The brake cylinder pressure should drop by approximately 5lb/psi and then climb to 25lb/psi so as to compensate for the changeover between E.P. and auto.
- The brake should then be gradually applied until full service is reached at approximately 50lb/psi.
- The brake handle should then be smartly placed to the emergency position. As the brake pipe vents to '0', the brake cylinder should remain at 50lb/psi. Lastly, the brake handle should be placed in the release position to re-charge the brake Pipe.
- Select E.P. brake on the selector switch and leave approximately 10 to 20lb/psi in the brake cylinders to hold the unit still.

D.S.D. test:

- Let go of the D.S.D./power handle with the reverser in the forward position. The brake pipe should vent to '0' and the brake cylinder should charge to approximately 50lb/psi.
- Replace the D.S.D. and put the reverser back to neutral. The brake pipe should recharge to a minimum of 65lb/psi and the brake cylinder should return to approximately 10 to 20lb/psi.

GUARD'S BRAKE TEST

- The guard must carry out the test from a cab or brake van, depending upon circumstances of the brake test required, i.e. at the beginning of a journey or when an attachment/detachment has been made between units.
- A full Service E.P. brake application is applied by the driver. The guard observes that the brake cylinder pressure rises to approximately 50lb/psi before the driver reduces the brake to approximately 10 to 20lb/psi.
- The guard then vents the brake pipe by using the emergency brake/brake handle. The driver should observe the brake cylinder rising to approximately 50lb/psi and the brake pipe falling to '0.'
- The guard then replaces the brake handle and the driver observes that the brake pipe charges to a minimum of 65lb/psi while the brake cylinder returns to approximately 10 to 20lb/psi.

RUNNING BRAKE TEST

- To be carried out as appropriate, i.e. at the beginning of a journey, before the first crossover when leaving sidings or a terminus, before a steep falling gradient, or during fog or falling snow.
- The driver places the brake selector switch to auto and then applies a gentle brake application which is just enough to feel a reduction in speed. The brakes are then released and the brake selector switch is replaced to E.P.

SHUTTING DOWN THE DRIVING CAB

A driver would carry out the following procedure when changing ends or before berthing a train in sidings or sheds etc. No handbrake could be applied when a driver changed ends and so the procedure trapped air in the brake cylinders to hold the train still. The handbrake would always be applied when berthing a train.

- Place the brake handle to full service. The brake cylinder should charge to approximately 50lb/psi.
- Place the brake selector switch to auto.
- Place the brake handle to emergency. The brake pipe should fall to '0'.
- Turn the master switch off and remove the E.P. key (This traps the air in the brake cylinders).
- Place the brake handle in the release position and observe that approximately 50lb/psi remains in the brake cylinders.
- Turn the headlight off, put headcode to 'red blanks' and apply the handbrake if necessary.

Further reading

Brown, D. *Southern Electric, Development of the London suburban network and its trains,* Capital Transport, 2009

Brown, D. *Southern Electric, Main line electrification, the war years and British Railways,* Capital Transport, 2010

Butlin, A. *British Multiple Units: Volume 4 Classes 410 – 490 & 508,* Coorlea Publishing, 2004

Hall, S. *ABC Modern Signalling Handbook, revised 4th edition,* Ian Allan, 2010

Oliver, B. *British Railways Southern Region Electrics in Colour, for the Modeller and Historian,* Ian Allan, 2008

Oliver, B. *Southern EMUs before Privatisation in Colour, for the Modeller and Historian,* Ian Allan, 2010

Oliver, B. *Southern EMUs since Privatisation in Colour, for the Modeller and Historian,* Ian Allan, 2011

Taylor, R. *Train driver, a Railway Career Memoir,* Warners Group Publications plc, 2009

Vent, A.P. *Sussex Motorman, the Hubert Hobden Memoirs, Volume 2, 1935-1961,* Buggleskelly Books, 2009

Recommended DVD titles

Bognor Regis to London Victoria, 225 Studios, class 377 EMU

Brighton to Portsmouth Harbour, 225 Studios, 4 CIG EMU

Cab rides around the British Isles No.29, Brighton to London Victoria, Railway Recollections, 4 BIG EMU

Connex express, Video 125, Class 319 EMU

East Coastway and Marshlink, Video 125, 170 Turbostar and 377 EMU

End of the Slam Door Train, NM Productions

Filmed by Ashley Barton at Lover's Walk depot. There is a 'walk through' of a 4 CIG and a 4 VEP unit, both filmed during the last days of slam door units. This DVD is available from the Network SouthEast Railway Society.

Final years of the 'Slam Door' EMUs, Train Crazy, 100 minutes

1066 DC, Hastings to Charing Cross, Video 125, 4 CEP EMU

Havant to Bournemouth, 225 Studios, 4 CIG EMU

Journey to Hastings, 225 Studios, 4 CIG EMU

Southern Electric, Transport Video Publishing

Southern Suburban, 225 Studios, class 377 and 455 EMUs